Seafood Grilling

Twice a Week

Acknowledgments

Editor: **Kari Petersen**
Design and Production: **Fusion Studios**
Illustrations: **Al Tietjen**
Nutritional Review: **Cindy Snyder MPH, RD**

Alaska Seafood Marketing Institute
California Seafood Council
Maine Lobster Marketing Council
North Carolina State University
Seafood Producers Cooperative
University of Washington
Western Fishboat Owners Association

Published by **National Seafood Educators**

Seafood Grilling

Twice a Week

by
Evie Hansen

SEAFOOD
TWICE A WEEK

National Seafood Educators • Richmond Beach, Washington

Inquiries should be addressed to:
Permissions Department
National Seafood Educators
P.O. Box 60006
Richmond Beach, WA 98160
PH: (206) 546-6410
FX: (206) 546-6411
Email: eviense@aol.com

Printed and bound in the United States of America
6th Printing — 2004

ISBN: 0-9616426-5-3

Library of Congress Catalog Publication Data
Hansen, Evie
Seafood Grilling Twice A Week/Evie Hansen
        p.   cm.
Includes bibliographical references and index.
1. Seafood 2. Cookery (seafood) 3. Health-Nutritional aspects
TX747.H347   2001
641.6'92   QBJ97-40214

To Mom and Dad, who gave me the
most wonderful childhood any kid
could ask for.

To my mother- and father-in-law,
who gave me the most wonderful
husband on earth.

Contents

Chapter 1: Nutrition

Chapter 2: Safety

Chapter 3: Preparation

Chapter 4: At the Grill

x

Preface

Seafood grillin' was always a fun time at home. Dad would bring home his catch of the day, and Mom would perform her magic on the grill. What added to the excitement was the uncertainty of what kind of fish it would be: lingcod, salmon, halibut, mackerel, albacore tuna, or maybe an assortment of rockfish. Mom's magic exploded when the fresh herbs were picked from our huge garden to toss on the grilling fish.

I graduated to head griller at our wedding for 500 guests. We served barbecued wild king salmon, which Dad caught on his commercial fishing troller. I have been grilling seafood ever since, preparing whatever catch my husband, brother, or father brings home. Some of the best grilling times have come on vacation when I go to the nearest market and use its local seafood, herbs, and seasonings.

Presented here are some unusual and interesting ways to grill fish and shellfish. They are intended to renew your enthusiasm for seafood cookery and to show you how grilling seafood can be easy, tasty, and healthy. My hope is that you will be inspired to make these recipes your own with your regional grilling secrets.

Bring home your catch from the market or boat and start grilling seafood twice a week. You'll be glad you did!

—Evie Hansen

Introduction

No one seems to know specifically when grilling first came into practice. It's quite possible Adam and Eve grilled St. Peter's fish (now called tilapia) over applewood coals in the Garden of Eden. Whatever the situation, we can assume that the first person to throw his or her hunk of meat onto a bed of hot coals quickly realized how tender and juicy this form of cooking made the meat.

Since then, grilling has come a long way, yet not far at all—if you don't want it to. The beauty of this ancient culinary art is that it can be just as satisfying today as it was thousands of years ago—and that even if time and conditions are limited, grilled food can still be easy to prepare, delectably quick, and convenient. We can travel from the simple to the extravagant. It is the variables—from the weather to the company, from the kind of food to your frame of mind—that make each grilling experience uniquely gratifying.

Today the possibilities are virtually limitless. The joy of all the options—from beachside bonfires to indoor rotisseries—allows us to delight in grilling not only on a summer Sunday afternoon, but also every other day of the week and throughout the entire year! Our tongs and spatulas no longer have to leave when the sun does.

Grilling is one of America's favorite cooking pastimes. People no longer want to limit grilling to family reunions and the Super Bowl. And, more specifically, people no longer want to limit grilling *seafood* to family reunions and the Super Bowl. You will quickly learn, if you don't already know, that grilled seafood will make any meal a special occasion!

People often enjoy grilling because everyone can be involved in the open-air interaction between food and fire. Everyone can participate in the grilling process by being in charge of different parts of the meal. Entire meals can be prepared on the grill—appetizers through desserts!

We are confident that within this book you will find many reasons to keep returning to these pages. Our goal is to provide you with inspiration that leads to confidence and enthusiasm. We have written the book in such a way that it can be either a foolproof guide that you follow to the letter, or a springboard to launch you on the path to your own creations and concoctions. Either way, you will learn how to become a backyard hero.

Before we instruct you in the art of grilling, however, we discuss a few basics that are essential in preparing an easy, fun, and delectable meal. We begin by reviewing the tremendous health benefits of seafood. Next, we carefully and thoroughly walk you through the steps you need to follow to ensure that you are using safe seafood. Do not skip these important details. Following these sections, we discuss grill types, procedures, styles, and techniques. Then we dive into the recipes! Each one suggests seafood substitutions, so you can go seafood shopping and bring home what is in season or on sale.

We know you would rather spend your time enjoying your company and the experience of grilling than trying to interpret a recipe, so we have endeavored to provide simple, clear instructions. Our recipes feature the fish most commonly found in seafood markets or sport-caught in North America. All of the ingredients needed for our recipes are available at the supermarket. Each recipe is kitchen-tested, and most have a cooking time of 20 minutes or less. You will not be disappointed in either the taste or the health benefits seafood provides.

We present many options and tips for grilling seafood, but remember that when the game clock starts, you are the captain, and you will be calling the shots according to what works best for you. There are no absolutes . . . except that it is time to make some down-home, lighthearted, divinely grilled seafood!

Kari Petersen
Editor

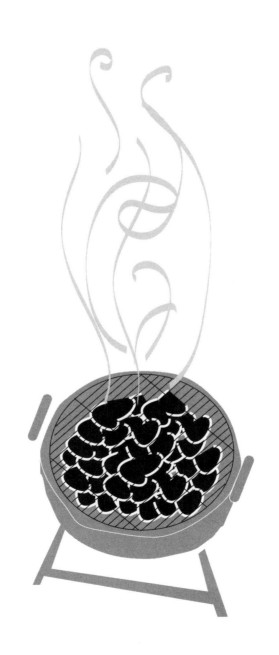

Chapter 1
Nutrition

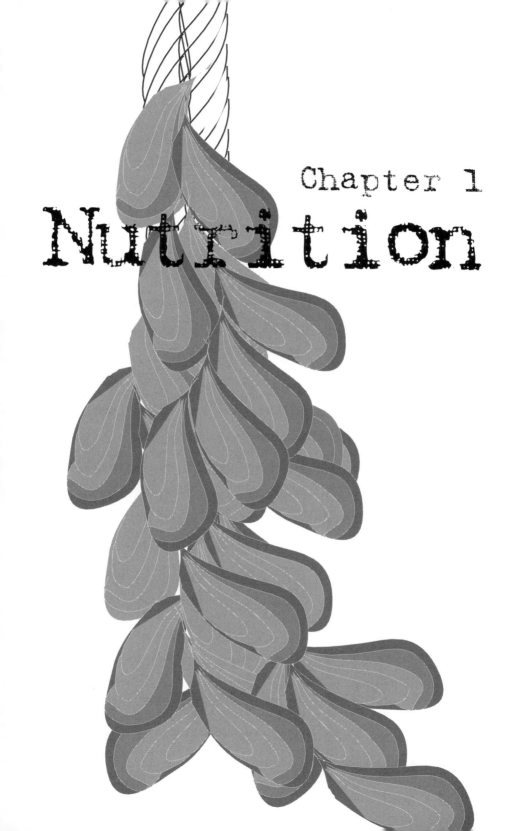

Nutrition

Dietary Guidelines for Americans

Americans are increasingly faced with health concerns and illnesses, and people are searching for preventive measures that can help build strong bodies and reduce certain chronic diseases. Nutrition is an area we can control, and good nutrition is not as hard to come by as it used to be. A variety of food choices are available that can meet the needs of different lifestyles, taste preferences, and dietary restrictions. Healthy eating and regular physical activity help enable people of all ages to feel their best and strive toward healthy, happy living.

Recently the United States Department of Agriculture (USDA) and the Department of Health and Human Services issued a report, *Dietary Guidelines for Americans, 2000*, encouraging Americans to aim for optimal health. The report's basic ABC message speaks to you and your family.

Aim for fitness.

Build a healthy base.

Choose sensibly.

These recommendations are intended for healthy children (ages 2 and older) and adults of any age.

Aim for Fitness

- Aim for a healthy weight.
- Be physically active each day.

Build a Healthy Base

- Let the Pyramid guide your food choices.
- Choose a variety of grains daily, especially whole grains.
- Choose a variety of fruits and vegetables daily.
- Keep food safe to eat.

Choose Sensibly

- Choose a diet that is low in saturated fat and cholesterol and moderate in total fat.
- Choose beverages and foods that limit your intake of sugars.
- Choose and prepare foods with less salt.
- If you drink alcoholic beverages, do so in moderation.

The USDA's report also states that all kinds of unsaturated fats (oils) help keep blood cholesterol low. Unsaturated fats occur in fatty fish such as salmon, among other foods. According to the USDA, fatty ocean fish also have a special type of polyunsaturated fat (omega-3 fatty acids) that may protect against heart disease. And most important for the grill fans among us, the USDA recommends grilling foods, such as fish, as opposed to frying them.

So if you are looking for healthy foods and smart ways to prepare them, this book couldn't be more perfect for you and your family!

Recommendations from Leading Health Organizations

The following guidelines were developed for the U.S. population (ages 2 and older); however, people with a history of health problems may need to adjust them.

Total fat: No more than 30 percent of total calories
> **Saturated fatty acids:** 8 to 10 percent of total calories
> **Polyunsaturated fatty acids:** Up to 10 percent of total calories
> **Monounsaturated fatty acids:** 15 percent of total calories
> Most seafood provides a fraction of the recommended percentage of fat intake. For example, a 3-ounce serving of one of the oiliest fish, Atlantic mackerel, has less than 25 percent of the 67 grams of total fat allowed for a person who consumes 2,000 calories a day. The vast majority of seafood has considerably less fat than that. Many species of seafood have less than one gram of fat per $3\frac{1}{2}$-ounce serving! Remember, however, that the fat contained in seafood is the "good" fat—polyunsaturated—and is rich in omega-3's.

Cholesterol: Less than 300 milligrams per day
> Cholesterol levels are low in most seafood, with an average of 15 to 20 mg of cholesterol per ounce. Compare that to 25 mg per ounce for chicken and 30 mg per ounce for beef. The cholesterol content of shellfish varies depending upon whether the fish is a mollusk or a crustacean. Mollusks—clams, mussels, oysters—are vegetarians (they eat sea plants), so they tend to have less cholesterol. Crustaceans—shrimp, lobsters, crabs—eat small animals, so they contain higher levels of cholesterol. However, some studies have found that eating crustaceans has no effect on cholesterol levels.

Sodium: Less than 2,400 milligrams per day (equivalent to $1\frac{1}{2}$ teaspoons of salt)
> Seafood, especially saltwater seafood, is naturally low in sodium. A $3\frac{1}{2}$-ounce serving of finfish provides less than 100 mg per ounce.

Carbohydrates: 55 to 60 percent of total calories (emphasize complex carbohydrates)

Total calories: Dependent on each individual (adjusted to achieve and maintain a healthy body weight)

Seafood is the best protein investment for the calorie-conscious consumer. Most seafood contains less than 100 calories in a $3\frac{1}{2}$-ounce serving. Compare that with 160 calories for a similar portion of chicken and more than 200 calories for beef. A $3\frac{1}{2}$-ounce fillet of sole will fill half of your plate for only 90 calories! Plus, because of the rich and delicate flavor of seafood, it's not necessary to add other fats and oils to increase flavor. This keeps the cooking process low in calories as well.

Protein: 10 to 20 percent of total calories

An average $3\frac{1}{2}$-ounce serving of seafood provides 17 to 21 grams of complete protein, which is about half the protein the body needs each day. In addition, because seafood does not contain much connective tissue, it is easier to chew and digest than most other protein choices.

Variety: Eat a variety of foods

The best advice is to eat more of all types of finfish and shellfish.

Exercise: Be at least moderately active for 30 minutes (or more) 4 to 5 days a week

Alcohol: Limit consumption. Don't "drink like a fish"!

Nutritional Benefits of Seafood

For more than a decade now, fish and shellfish have been capturing health headlines with their startling nutritional value. Study after study has revealed the health benefits of seafood . . . and the list keeps growing. We are still finding new benefits of making seafood a regular part of our diet.

The attention began over twenty-five years ago, when researchers noticed two different large populations that clearly had significantly low (in fact, almost nonexistent) levels of heart disease. First, researchers found that the Eskimos of Greenland—who consumed large amounts of fish high in polyunsaturated fatty acids (omega-3's)—had almost no heart disease within their population due to the protective benefits of omega-3's. Second, the Japanese, who also rely heavily on fish as a mainstay of their diet, were observed to have a low rate of heart attacks. In addition, the same seemed true of Scandinavians, Dutch, and even Americans who consumed regular amounts of seafood. The studies did not end there, however; that was just the beginning.

What Are Omega-3's?

Omega-3 fatty acids are a family of particularly long-chained polyunsaturated fats that share a unique chemical structure. These fats are even more unsaturated than vegetable oil. Among the seven members of the omega-3 family, the two most prominent are eicosapentaenoic acid (EPA) and docosahexaenoic acid (DHA). Nutritional values for omega-3 fatty acids generally represent the sum of EPA and DHA.

Omega-3's reside plentifully in seafood, especially in the "fattier" types of fish. Keep in mind, however, that this is "good" fat because it is unsaturated. We call these fatty acids unique because they are not found in very many foods. By far, seafood contains the largest amount of omega-3's.

How Much Should I Eat?

The U.S. government has not yet seen fit to devise a recommended intake of omega-3 fatty acids, although all nutritionists agree there should be one. In fact, several other countries have already issued official recommendations for omega-3 consumption. Many experts within this field expect that the U.S. government will soon develop similar guidelines and recognize omega-3 as an essential nutrient. The USDA/HHS report *Dietary Guidelines for Americans, 2000* states, "There is a need to investigate optimal ratios of saturated-to-monounsaturated-to-polyunsaturated fats, including ratios of omega-6 to omega-3 fatty acids. The potential for omega-3 polyunsaturated fat to reduce the risks for cardiovascular diseases and cancer deserves particular attention."

Although the U.S. government has yet to act on this issue, the available research suggests that most of us would do well to eat more fish and shellfish. The U.S. Surgeon General and the American Heart Association have been urging Americans to eat more fish and make it a regular part of our diet. There is a common understanding among doctors and nutritionists that people should eat seafood at least twice a week to obtain enough omega-3's for long-lasting benefits.

Omega-3's and Your Family

It is now clear to scientists that we need omega-3's for proper brain and eye development, and that they are an essential nutrient for babies. As babies grow, their brains and nervous systems begin accumulating DHA (one of the fish omega-3's). DHA is used for building brain tissue, for nerve growth, and for the development of the eye's retina. A mother who eats plenty of fish will give her baby generous amounts of DHA by nourishing the unborn child through her body and by breast-feeding. Babies not breast-fed will be deprived of DHA unless it is supplied through a fish oil–supplemented formula.

At a recent omega-3 conference held in Washington, D.C., scientists showed that premature infants have less DHA in their tissues than full-term infants. Nutrition expert Cindy Snyder says that regular seafood consumption during pregnancy can prolong gestation, reducing incidence of premature birth and increasing mean birth weight. We need to be encouraging greater seafood consumption by pregnant and nursing women, as well as feeding our young children more seafood.

Additional Health Benefits

- In one of many studies that have found similar results, researchers at Boston's Brigham and Women's Hospital in 1996 documented a 50 percent reduced risk of cardiac arrest in subjects who ate at least one fish meal per week, when compared with subjects who ate only one fish meal per month.
- Omega-3 fatty acids have been shown to protect against heart disease in a variety of ways:
  - Omega-3's inhibit the formation of blood clots, which can often lead to heart attacks.
  - Omega-3's may prevent deadly heartbeat abnormalities that can cause sudden cardiac arrest.
  - Omega-3's lower very high levels of triglycerides, which can increase the risk of heart attacks when elevated.
  - Omega-3's may restrict growth of plaque that narrows arteries leading to the heart.
- Ongoing studies by Dr. Joel Kremer of New York's Albany Medical College show omega-3's to be improving tender joints and reducing morning stiffness in rheumatoid arthritis patients.
- The research of Bruce Watkins at Purdue University suggests that omega-3's improve bone growth, which is of crucial value to young children.
- Some studies suggest that eating fish can lower cholesterol. Seafood is low in cholesterol (with the exception of some shellfish, which contain moderate levels).
- Eating fatty fish regularly has been shown to modestly lower blood pressure.
- Because of the anti-inflammatory properties of omega-3's, they may dampen the inflammatory activity in the immune system that is thought to promote Alzheimer's disease.
- Eating fish can reduce the damage to the kidneys that occurs in severe insulin-dependent diabetes.

For all these reasons, and still more to come, seafood is a healthy food. Eating two seafood meals per week will provide a protective health benefit to you and those you serve it to. And seafood is as delicious as it is healthy! Grilling is perfect for seafood since it requires little or no added fat for flavor, and imparts a flavor all its own as well. Grilling is the perfect way to naturally and deliciously prepare your seafood.

Safe and Informed Grilling

Lately there has been an increasing concern about the possible health dangers associated with grilling. We know that two kinds of chemicals are created during grilling: polycyclic aromatic hydrocarbons (PAHs) and heterocyclic amines (HCAs). PAHs are formed when fat drips down onto an open flame and sends up a stream of smoke, coating the food with carcinogens. HCAs are created when meats are cooked at a high heat until well done. The food's amino acids react with creatine (a chemical in muscle meats) to produce HCAs. Research has shown that in animals, either of these chemicals can cause the kind of genetic mutations that result in cancer. Though studies have not shown this to be true in humans, there is plenty of suspicion.

The good news is that there are many things you can do to eliminate or reduce the amount of PAHs and HCAs touching your food. The following techniques are recommended by the Mayo Clinic and many others.

- Reduce fat drippings by grilling fish, lean meats, or skinless poultry.
- Use low-fat marinades to minimize fire flare-ups. Though the process is not completely understood, marinades are believed to cut HCAs by up to 90 percent by drawing out the chemical precursors of the carcinogens.
- Keep grilling time to a minimum.
- To reduce flare-ups, avoid piercing the food with forks—use long tongs to turn the meat.
- Cook food on a sheet of foil to reduce direct smoke exposure.
- Remove charred portions from cooked food.

We are happy to say that all of these issues can be directly addressed in regard to seafood!

- Most seafood is low in fat and produces very little, if any, drippings during grilling.
- We use a variety of low-fat marinades in the majority of our recipes, resulting in very few flare-ups.
- We have recommended in Chapter 4, *At the Grill*, that you use tongs to turn food, not only to reduce flare-ups but also because you don't want to pierce the meat and lose those succulent juices that are trapped inside!
- Due to the small amount of connective tissue in seafood, cooking times are very short; so very little time over the grill is required.
- When filleted, dressed, or whole fish are grilled, the skin acts as a protective barrier. In the same way, the shells of shrimp, crab, and lobster shield the food you eat from any chemicals produced in grilling. If you like, you can place foil underneath your food; many of our recipes call for the use of foil.
- Seafood should never be charred! Fish is never better well-done—that's just considered overdone. If you did not hear your timer over the screaming of the children, remove all charred portions of the seafood. Luckily, usually only the skin or shell of the seafood gets charred, so no "food" is lost!

We do not want you to fear throwing your fish on the backyard grill, but we do want you to be cautious and educated about how you can prevent adverse health effects.

Nutritional Comparisons

All values per 3.5 oz. (100 gm) raw edible portion	Calories	Protein (gm)	Total Fat (gm)	Omega-3 (gm)	Saturated Fat (gm)	Cholesterol (mg)	Sodium (mg)
Anchovy	130	20	5	1.5	1	60	105
Arctic Char	180	22	8	1.0	2	25	80
Bass - Chilean Sea	185	13	14	1.3	3	50	55
Freshwater	115	19	4	0.6	1	70	70
Striped	95	18	2	0.8	0.5	80	70
Bluefish	125	20	4	0.8	1	60	60
Catfish - Farm-raised	135	16	8	0.3	2	45	55
Wild	95	16	3	0.4	0.5	60	45
Cod - Atlantic	80	18	1	0.2	0.0	45	55
Pacific	80	18	1	0.2	0.0	35	70
Croaker, Atlantic	105	18	3	0.2	1	60	55
Flounder	90	19	1	0.2	0.5	50	80
Grouper	90	19	1	0.3	0.0	35	55
Haddock	85	19	1	0.2	0.0	55	70
Hake (Whiting)	85	16	2	0.4	0.0	N/A	85
Halibut	110	21	2	0.3	0.5	30	55
Herring - Atlantic	160	18	9	1.6	2	60	90
Pacific	195	16	14	1.7	3.5	75	75
Hoki	80	17	2	0.3	N/A	30	95
Lingcod	85	18	1	0.0	0.0	50	60
Mackerel - Atlantic	205	19	14	2.3	3.5	70	90
King	105	20	2	0.3	0.5	50	160
Pacific (Jack)	160	20	8	1.4	2	45	85
Spanish	140	19	6	1.4	2	75	60
Mahi-mahi	90	19	1	N/A	0.0	85	130
Monkfish	75	15	2	N/A	N/A	25	20
Mullet	115	19	4	0.3	1	50	65
Orange Roughy	70	15	1	0.0	0.0	20	65
Perch	90	19	1	0.3	0.0	90	60
Pike - Northern	90	19	1	0.1	0.0	40	40
Walleye	95	19	1	0.3	0.0	85	50
Pollock - Alaska	80	17	1	0.4	0.0	70	100
Atlantic	90	19	1	0.4	0.0	70	85
Pompano	165	18	10	0.6	3.5	50	65
Rockfish	95	19	2	0.3	0.5	35	60
Sablefish (Black Cod)	195	13	15	1.4	3	50	55
Salmon							
Atlantic, Farm-raised	183	20	11	1.9	2	60	60
King (Chinook), Wild	180	20	10	1.4	2.5	65	45
Chum, Wild	120	20	4	0.6	1	75	50
Coho (Silver), Wild	145	22	6	1.1	1.5	45	45
Pink, Wild	115	20	4	1.0	0.5	50	65
Sockeye (Red), Wild	170	21	9	1.2	1.5	60	45
Sardine (see Pacific Herring)							

FINFISH

Nutritional Comparisons

All values per 3.5 oz. (100 gm) raw edible portion	Calories	Protein (gm)	Total Fat (gm)	Omega-3 (gm)	Saturated Fat (gm)	Cholesterol (mg)	Sodium (mg)
FINFISH							
Sea Bass	95	18	2	0.6	0.5	40	70
Shark	130	21	5	0.9	1	50	80
Dogfish	165	15	11	1.9	4	45	100
Mako	125	18	8	0.9	1	50	80
Skate	95	21	1	N/A	N/A	N/A	N/A
Smelt	95	18	2	0.7	0.5	70	60
Snapper	100	21	1	0.3	0.5	35	65
Sole	90	19	1	0.2	0.5	50	80
Sturgeon	105	16	4	0.3	1	60	55
Surimi	100	15	1	N/A	0.0	30	145
Swordfish	120	20	4	0.6	1	40	90
Tilapia	85	18	1	N/A	0.5	50	35
Tilefish	95	18	2	0.4	0.5	50	55
Trout - Rainbow							
Farm-raised	140	21	5	0.9	1.5	60	35
Rainbow, Wild	120	21	4	0.6	0.5	60	30
Seatrout	105	17	4	0.4	1	85	60
Tuna - Albacore	170	25	7	2.1	2	40	50
Bluefin	145	23	5	1.2	1.5	40	40
Skipjack	105	22	1	0.3	0.5	45	35
Yellowfin	110	23	1	0.2	0.0	45	35
Turbot	95	16	3	N/A	1	50	150
Wahoo	125	24	2	N/A	N/A	N/A	80
Whitefish	135	19	6	1.3	1	60	50
Whiting	90	18	1	0.2	0.0	65	70
CRUSTACEANS							
Crab - Blue	85	18	1	0.3	0.0	80	295
Dungeness	85	17	1	0.3	0.0	60	295
Imitation	100	12	1	0.6	0.5	20	840
King	85	18	1	N/A	0.0	40	835
Snow	90	18	1	0.4	0.0	55	540
Crayfish	75	16	1	0.1	0.0	115	60
Lobster - American	90	19	1	0.0	0.0	95	295
Spiny	110	21	2	0.4	0.0	70	175
Shrimp, All Varieties	105	20	2	0.5	0.5	150	150
MOLLUSKS							
Abalone	105	17	1	0.1	0.0	85	300
Clams	75	13	1	0.1	0.0	35	55
Mussels, Blue	85	12	2	0.4	0.5	30	285
Octopus	80	15	1	0.2	0.0	50	230
Oysters - Eastern	70	7	3	0.6	1	55	210
Pacific	80	10	2	0.7	0.5	50	105
Scallops	90	17	1	0.2	0.0	35	160
Squid	90	16	1	0.5	0.5	235	45

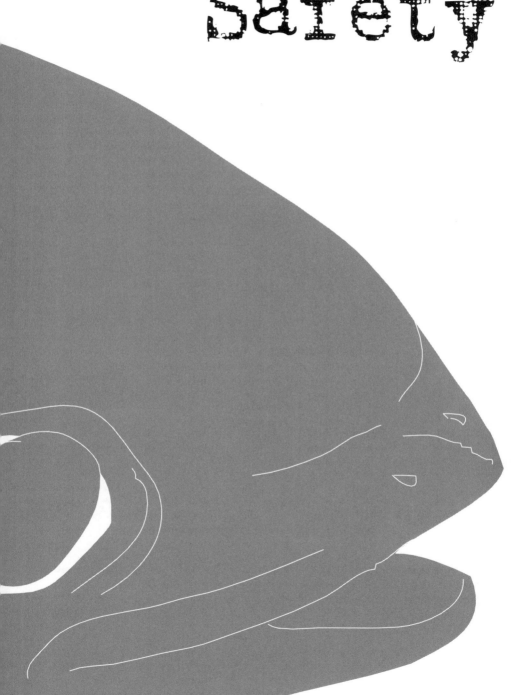

Chapter 2
Safety

Safety

The best protection you have against food-borne illnesses is to realize that any food has the potential to cause an illness if it is not stored, handled, and cooked properly. In 1994, more than 220,000 people got sick from eating ice cream. Ice cream! Every food has the potential for bacterial growth. However, instead of fearing food, realize that education is your greatest defense.

To begin, we will teach you what the government is doing to ensure that seafood is taken from the water safely and healthily and arrives in the retailer's hands the same way. Next, we will inform you on how to buy great seafood, store it at home (whether in the refrigerator or freezer), prepare it safely, and grill it to perfection. These detailed step-by-step guidelines will provide you with the information necessary to enjoy making seafood a regular part of your home-prepared meals. You can control your kitchen and the seafood in it.

Seafood Safety Facts:

The Center for Food Safety of the U.S. Food and Drug Administration (FDA) conducted a study in 1991 that found the following rates of food-related illnesses:
- One illness per 1,000,000 servings of cooked seafood
- One illness per 250,000 servings of shellfish—including raw shellfish
- One illness for every 25,000 servings of chicken

Major Causes of Seafood Illnesses:
- Seafood captured illegally from contaminated waters
- Raw or undercooked seafood, especially oysters, clams, and mussels
- Seafood contaminated by improper handling in the home or a food service establishment

You, too, can adopt safe seafood-handling practices to minimize your risk of developing a seafood-related illness. These are all areas over which you have a great deal of control. You can claim your kitchen as a "Safe Seafood Zone"!

Government Actions to Protect the Consumer

Always buy your seafood from a reputable source. Avoid the temptation to buy seafood from a roadside stand—even if the sign is screaming "FRESH!"—or you might get more than you bargained for. Seafood products that move through traditional commercial channels are monitored by the government in the following ways to ensure safety.

1. The National Shellfish Sanitation Program (NSSP) continually monitors shellfish-harvesting waters for the presence of pollutants and environmental

contaminants. Shellfish that have received governmental approval are labeled with a certification tag, which identifies the location of harvest. A reputable seafood salesperson will purchase shellfish only from approved waters and will gladly show you certification tags upon request.

2. The Food and Drug Administration (FDA) inspects seafood processors, shippers, packers, labelers, and warehouses to ensure that they maintain good manufacturing practices. The FDA also monitors the quality of the products. When seafood does not meet FDA standards, it can be removed from interstate commerce.

3. The FDA also oversees the voluntary inspection program known as HACCP (Hazard Analysis and Critical Control Point). The HACCP system involves identifying and monitoring "critical points" in handling and processing seafood where the risk of contamination is the greatest. Seafood plants design their own HACCP plans and submit them to the FDA for approval. The FDA monitors the implementation of these plans.

4. The FDA has set "action levels" for a number of chemical contaminants. State agencies are responsible for sampling suspected species. If contaminant levels exceed FDA limits, fishing of that species will be forbidden.

5. Since over 50 percent of U.S. seafood is imported, the FDA monitors the quality of imported fish. Many foreign countries sign agreements to comply with U.S. safety standards.

6. Most commercially caught fish is captured offshore in clean, deep-sea waters. However, about 20 percent of all seafood eaten in the United States is derived from recreational or subsistence fishing. Very little of this fish shows up in the retail market. State and local governments regulate the status of fishing waters to ensure safety for recreational anglers.

Purchasing Safe Seafood

Evaluating a Seafood Counter

If you are new to the area, or new to buying seafood in your area, begin by asking your trusted friends and relatives for recommendations of the best local seafood counters. Referrals are always a great place to start!

Then go visit the counters. But if you smell a counter before you see it, turn around and walk away. Cleanliness *is* next to godliness, especially at a seafood counter. Below are some more tips to follow on your visits.

Stand back from the counter and look at it:

- The employees handling the seafood should be clean. They should not be smoking, eating, playing with their hair, or sick; they should not have any open wounds. They should be wearing gloves, and should change them between touching raw seafood and moving to cooked foods or to nonfood tasks.
- The displays should be properly cooled (iced), to 32°F.

- Fish should be displayed on a thick bed of fresh (not melting) ice, preferably in a case or under some type of cover.
- There should be no cross-contamination (no cooked seafood touching raw seafood).
- Fish should not be displayed in the same case as red meat, which has a different storage temperature.
- Product signs, price markers, and so on should not be stuck into the fish. (This introduces spoilage bacteria.)
- Finally, watch other shoppers and notice what they are buying. Then ask them why!

Ask your retailer these questions:
- What is the freshest or is freshly frozen today?
- Where did it come from?
- How was it caught?
- When was it caught?
- Would you serve this to your family?
- Are there certain days of the week that the seafood is freshest or has the greatest variety (shipment days)?
- Do they guarantee that their seafood is safe and of good quality? Every store should.

Then look closely at the seafood itself. Remember, be flexible when going to the store; buy the freshest fish, even if that is not the type you had originally planned on purchasing. We've included a list of substitution suggestions at the top of each recipe, as well as a *Seafood Substitution Chart* in Chapter 3, to help guide you.

A final note: Compliment the retailer if your dinner is a success. Compliments will encourage the staff to do their job well!

Seafood Counter Evaluation Checklist

FRESH WHOLE, DRESSED, OR DRAWN FISH

Good Quality	Poor Quality
Clear, bright, bulging eyes (Walleye pike have cloudy eyes.)	Dull, cloudy, sunken, bloody eyes
Bright-red gills	Brown or grayish gills, white slime
Flesh firm, springs back when pressed	Soft, flabby flesh separating from bone
Ocean-fresh, slight seaweed odor	Sour, ammonia-like fishy odor
Scales tightly adhered to skin	Dull or missing areas
Belly cavity (if gutted) clean, no blood or viscera	Belly cavity (if gutted) with traces of blood or viscera

FRESH FILLETS, STEAKS, & LOINS

Good Quality	Poor Quality
Bright, consistent coloring, almost translucent	Flesh bruised, brown at the edges, irregular color, rainbow opalescence
Ocean-fresh, slight seaweed odor	Sour, ammonia-like odor
Firm, elastic flesh (springs back when pressed)	Soft, mushy flesh
Clean cut edges, evenly trimmed	Tears, ragged edges
Moist but not slimy	Dry or slimy

LIVE CRAB, LOBSTER, SHRIMP, & OTHER CRUSTACEANS

Good Quality	Poor Quality
Lively legs, move when touched	Little or no movement
Hard shell (unless soft-shelled variety)	Soft shells (harvested before molt is done)
Heavy weight (means there is more meat)	Light for size
Live lobster tail curls under when lifted up	Tail hangs limp

LIVE CLAMS, MUSSELS, OYSTERS, SCALLOPS, & OTHER MOLLUSKS

Good Quality	Poor Quality
Shells tightly closed; if open, they shut when tapped	Open shells; do not shut when tapped
Shells intact, moist	Cracked, chipped, dry shells
Clean scent	Strong fishy odor

SHUCKED CLAMS, MUSSELS, OYSTERS, SCALLOPS, & OTHER MOLLUSKS

Good Quality	Poor Quality
Plump meat	Shriveled, dark, dry meat
Free of shell and sand particles	Shell and sand present
Clear liquid, less than 10% of volume	Cloudy, opaque juice
Clean scent	Strong fishy odor

FROZEN FISH & SHELLFISH

Good Quality	Poor Quality
Flesh is solidly frozen	Flesh is partially thawed
When thawed, pass same criteria as fresh	Signs of drying out such as papery edges
Tight, moisture-proof package	Packaging is torn, crushed on edges
Product visible, unmarred	Shows signs of ice crystals or freezer burn

RAW SHRIMP

Good Quality	Poor Quality
Translucent shells with grayish green, pinkish tan, or pink tint	Blackened edges or spots on shells (except spot prawns)
Closely fitting shell	Loose shell caused by shrinkage
Moist	Dry
Firm flesh	Soft flesh

COOKED SHRIMP, LOBSTERS, & CRABS

Good Quality	Poor Quality
Hard shells (bright-red for lobster)	Discolored, soft, or broken shells
Picked meat:	Picked meat: Any off-color or dried out
Lobster: snow-white with red tints	
Crab: white with red or brown tints	
Shrimp: pink tints	
No shell fragments or cartilage	Shell and cartilage fragments
Mild, sweet scent	Strong fishy odor

SURIMI (IMITATION CRAB)

Good Quality	Poor Quality
Clean, fresh scent	Sour odor
Pull date available	Age unknown
Firm flesh	Slimy flesh
Ingredients listed on package	Ingredients unknown

CANNED SEAFOOD

Good Quality	Poor Quality
Cans not dented	Cans dented or leaking
Vacuum seal	No vacuum seal

Safety at Home

for Purchased or Sport-Caught Fish and Shellfish

CHILL—CLEAN—SEPARATE—COOK

Now that you have purchased your seafood, your responsibility for safe handling begins. Make the four simple words above the rule around your kitchen.

Chill: Refrigerate Promptly

There is a temperature "danger zone" between the refrigeration and cooking processes that invites bacteria to grow (40°–140°F). Minimize the time your seafood spends in that danger zone. Keep your hot foods hot and your cold foods cold. It is essential to keep seafood below 40°F during the chilling process to prevent the multiplication of bacteria. At no point should you allow your seafood to rise above that temperature. Here's how!

- Minimize the time the seafood is out of refrigeration. Make the seafood counter your final stop before heading to the checkstand.
- Ask the retailer to wrap your sealed seafood selection in a plastic bag packed with ice; or carry a cooler with a cold gel pack in your car or boat, and place seafood inside.

Refrigerating

When you get home, decide whether to store your seafood in the refrigerator or freezer, depending on when you will be consuming it. Whichever you decide, do it immediately when you arrive home!

FISH

- Remove gills and guts.
- Immediately wash under cold water.
- Pat dry.
- Wrap in plastic wrap and store in airtight container.
- Ice body cavity of whole, dressed, or drawn fish.
- Drain off accumulated water daily.
- Store in coldest part of refrigerator (usually under the freezer or in the meat drawer) at 32°–40°F.
- Do not pack the refrigerator; cool air must circulate.
- Keep seafood chilled until ready to grill.
- Fish will keep 2 to 4 days.

LIVE SHELLFISH

Live saltwater shellfish will die if they come in contact with fresh water; they must remain alive until they are cooked!

- Immediately refrigerate in an open-top bowl or container, and cover with damp cloth or paper towel.
- Store in cool part of refrigerator at 32°–40°F.
- Live shellfish will keep 2 to 3 days.
- Wash *just before* cooking.

Leftovers

- Refrigerate leftover seafood as soon as possible after eating. All cooked seafood left at room temperature for 2 hours or more should be discarded.
- Leftover seafood can still be warm when placed in the refrigerator. However, if large, thick portions of food still remain, break them down into smaller pieces. This allows for quicker cooling in the refrigerator. Minimize the time the food is in the "danger zone."

Freezing

If you decide to freeze your fish, we recommend that you ask yourself these questions and prepare accordingly:

- What is the most convenient form of frozen seafood to cook for my family (steaks, fillets, roasts, whole)?
- What size packages are most suitable (for one, for two, for a family, for entertaining)?
- How will the fish be cooked? (For instance, if you'll be grilling, you'll want to leave the skin on.)

Short-term

Most refrigerator freezers do not get cold enough for long-term storage of fish, and auto-defrost cycles produce a fluctuating temperature that destroys the quality of seafood. For these reasons, seafood should be stored in refrigerator freezers for no longer than 2 weeks.

Long-term

If you want to freeze seafood long-term, you need a freezer that is consistently 0°F or below. Assuming its temperature stays at 0°F or below, seafood will keep up to 6 months.

- To wrap fish for the freezer, use wrapping materials that will keep out the oxygen and moisture, such as freezer paper, plastic wrap, or plastic bags.
- Alternatively, glaze fish for the freezer. Glazing thoroughly coats the fish in ice. You can do this by covering the fish with water in a clean milk carton or plastic bag with sealed top, or by individually glazing each fish or fillet. To individually glaze: Dip seafood in cold water. Lay flat on a cookie sheet. Place in freezer for 2 hours. Repeat process at least four times. A thick coating of ice will provide a strong protective layer for your fish.

- Label packages before putting them in the freezer. Here's an example of the information you will want to include.

Type of fish: salmon
Type of cut: steaks
Serving Size: 2 lbs.
Date: March 26, 2000

Thawing

- Thaw seafood in refrigerator (about 18 hours per pound),

or

- Wrap seafood in plastic bag and thaw by running cold water over bag,

or

- Microwave with on-off method. Set on Medium-Low (30% power or defrost setting). Microwave for 30 seconds, rest for 30 seconds, rotate. Repeat until nearly thawed but still very cold to the touch.
- Never defrost at room temperature!

Refreezing

If seafood thaws before it is needed, it can be refrozen. As long as you know it has been held in the refrigerator for no more than *one* day, go ahead and refreeze it. The quality of refrozen seafood will not be as good, but it is safe to eat. However, if there is any indication of spoilage, discard it.

Clean: Wash Hands and Surfaces Often

Be on the alert at all times for places where germs could come in contact with food and where bacteria could grow. The key point is to keep all surfaces clean while preparing and cooking; that goes for utensils, counters, cutting boards, platters, and hands. Germs can hitch a ride around your kitchen in many ways. Be a kitchen germ detective! Follow the germ trail in your home—from packaging to plate to sink.

- Wash! Wash! Wash! Wash surfaces thoroughly and use hot, soapy water. Wash each surface for at least 20 seconds.
- Wash hands before and after handling raw seafood, and after any potential germ contact: sneezing, coughing, touching a pet, using the bathroom, etc.
- Cover any cuts or sores on your hands with bandages.
- Whenever preparing raw seafood, fill a sink full of hot, soapy water. When you are done using an item, *immediately* place it in the water. This will reduce the temptation to reuse dishes and utensils. Remember to keep your water hot and use an antibacterial soap.

- Wash down the inside of your refrigerator where any raw seafood liquids may have leaked.
- Change sponges frequently.
- Use plastic or other nonporous cutting boards.
- Wipe down work surfaces with diluted bleach or other disinfectant.
- Rinse seafood with cold water and check for any unusual or suspicious odors before you begin grilling.
- Wash all utensils used to test or turn seafood early in grilling, when fish is uncooked, before using them again on your cooked seafood.
- Always place grilled seafood on a clean, unused plate.

Cleanup
- Thoroughly wash cutting boards and utensils after preparing seafood. Clean countertops.
- Sanitize sinks with cleanser.
- Wash your dishcloth and hand towels in the washer in the hot cycle after each seafood meal is prepared. Consider using paper towels to help with cleanup so you can just throw them away when you are done.

Separate: Do Not Cross-Contaminate

The most common cause of seafood-related problems in the home is cross-contamination. Cross-contamination occurs when raw seafood or seafood juices come in contact with cooked seafood or any other food that will not be cooked. This can be easily avoided by careful handling!

- The number one goal: Never let raw seafood come in contact with cooked seafood or other raw or cooked foods. This includes food juices!
- Always wash your hands after coming in contact with raw seafood, before you do anything else.
- Keep raw seafood separate from direct contact with other foods in your refrigerator.
- Store your seafood in a way that will prevent any liquid drippings from falling on the food below. Either place the seafood on the bottom shelf or lay the seafood in a pan that will catch any possible juices.
- Whenever possible, handle seafood last—after fruit and salads are stored in the refrigerator and the bread is set aside.
- Prepare raw seafood in a designated area—separate from other food preparation. A spot near the sink works well. Keep everything used to prepare raw seafood in that area.
- When preparing raw seafood, use a cutting board that has not been used with any other foods. When finished, immediately place the cutting board in a sink of hot, soapy water so you will not be tempted to use that board again before it is thoroughly cleaned.

- After cooking, transfer the cooked seafood onto a clean plate, never onto the same plate used to carry the raw seafood.
- Handle the marinade carefully. Avoid brushing marinade onto cooked fish if it has come in contact with uncooked fish. All of our grilling recipes suggest that you hold aside 2 to 3 tablespoons of marinade before adding seafood. The reserved marinade can be used to baste cooked seafood before serving. Remember to use a clean brush. Discard any leftover marinade that was in contact with the raw meat, or bring it to a rolling boil for 2 minutes before using it on cooked meat.
- Never store cooked and raw seafood together.

Cook: *Proper Temperatures*

The FDA's 1999 Food Code contains the following recommendations:
- Cook fish to an internal temperature of 145°F for 15 seconds.
- Cook stuffed fish to an internal temperature of 165°F for 15 seconds.
- Use an instant-read thermometer, and insert it into the thickest part of the fish to determine the internal temperature.
- Use the Canadian Department of Fisheries and Oceans' 10-minute rule to gauge the cooking time of fish.
  - Measure fish at its thickest point. If fish is stuffed or rolled, include the filling in your measurement.
  - Cook fish about 10 minutes per inch of thickness. For example, a 1-inch-thick fish fillet should be cooked for 10 minutes. Remember, these are just estimated cooking times. Seafood will be perfectly cooked when the flesh in the center has just begun to turn from transparent to opaque (or whiter) and is firm but moist. It should flake when tested with a fork.
- Thoroughly cook anything that comes in contact with raw seafood or seafood juices.

**MEASURING
A FILLET**

**MEASURING
A ROAST**

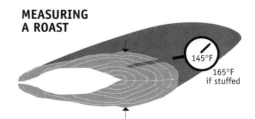

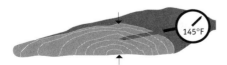

Measure fillet at thickest point. Cook 10 minutes per inch of thickness. To use thermometer, insert through side of fillet at thickest point.

Measure roast at thickest point. Cook 10 minutes per inch of thickness. To use thermometer, insert through side of roast at thickest point.

Safety at the Grill

Now that you have carefully selected your seafood, we know you are anxious to get grillin'. You can almost hear the dancing of fresh herbs on the coals, sending up pockets of tantalizing flavor. Just stick with me as we go over a few final safety tips with regard to the grill.

- Carefully read all instructions that come with your grilling unit.
- Keep your grill clean. Clean your pans after cooking; do not neglect your grill!
- Whether inside or out, be sure you have adequate ventilation.
- Position the grill in an open area well away from the house, covered decks, dry trees and leaves, and combustibles.
- Never leave a grill unattended, especially when children are present. Big dogs have been known to knock over grills, and cats have been known to leap on top, burning their paws. Always have someone tending the grill.
- Never allow children to operate a grill.
- Keep a fire extinguisher, bucket of sand, or source of water nearby.
- Do not wear loose clothes that could hang down and catch fire.
- Use appropriate tools (as discussed in Chapter 4, *At the Grill*).
- Have a water bottle filled with water on hand to shoot down flare-ups. Baking soda smothers grease flare-ups.
- If a fire occurs, cover the grill tightly (turn off burners if using a gas grill) and wait until flames subside.
- Keep all drip pans clean.

If using a charcoal grill:
- Use only fire starters that are certified for use on outdoor grills.
- Never add starter fluid or solid starters to coals that have already been ignited.
- Never use gasoline or other flammable liquids to ignite your grill.
- Check coals several hours later to be sure they are completely extinguished.

If using a gas grill:
- Open grill lid before lighting.
- Never store propane cylinders in an enclosed area, in direct sunlight, or within the reach of children.
- Always store propane cylinders upright.
- Make sure there are no sharp bends in the grill hoses.
- Occasionally check for cracks and leaks in the grill hoses. Applying suds from soapy water along the hose can help you locate any holes.
- Turn off the gas at the source after each use.

If using an indoor grill:
- Make sure that the grill can be used indoors.
- Never use propane or charcoal grills inside.
- Again, make sure you have adequate ventilation. Seafood is great for cooking indoors because of its short grilling time and small amount of fat, keeping smoke to a minimum.

Chapter 3
Preparation

Preparation

At The Store

Buying Tips

No one likes to pass up a good bargain, and we could all use tips on how to save a little extra money. This section provides some suggestions that are practical and helpful and will stretch your dollars.

- Here is a list of the 10 most common ingredients used throughout this book. You can prepare many of the recipes with just these ingredients. Be sure to add them to your cupboard if you do not already have them. You will be glad you did.
  - – extra-light olive oil
  - – salt
  - – pepper
  - – lemon juice
  - – lemon-pepper seasoning
  - – soy sauce
  - – garlic powder
  - – garlic cloves
  - – lime juice
  - – fresh ginger

- As you become accustomed to using these ingredients and your family learns to enjoy the flavors, you will want to explore the many choices on the grocery shelves. With vinegar, for instance, you can choose rice, balsamic, sweet, white, apple cider, or herb-flavored varieties. And remember, as you encounter recipes in this book that call for ingredients such as vinegar, you are not bound to use the specific flavor we recommend; the choice is yours.

- Check for seafood sales at your local retailer. Watch the papers for weekly specials. Usually some fish or shellfish is on sale, because whatever is in season will usually be available in abundance. With each recipe we supply a list of possible substitutions, allowing you to keep your options open with regard to what is freshest (or freshly frozen) and least expensive at the seafood counter. You can also refer to the *Seafood Substitution Chart* in this chapter.

- When you find a good bargain at the store, stock up! You can freeze the extra you will not be using in the next couple of days. Refer to Chapter 2, *Safety*, on how to safely freeze your seafood. It is always good to have some on hand.

- Purchase a whole fish, crab, lobster, or squid. Remember how Julia Child taught us to cut up a whole chicken? You can learn those same tips and save with seafood. A whole salmon can be made into steaks, fillets, and roasts for future dinners. Learning how to shake crabmeat out of the shell will help save money. The entire squid can be eaten, with the exception of the beak and innards; even the ink is highly prized. A little bit of labor will save you lots of money! Follow the ideas presented later in this chapter, in the *Grilling Cuts of Fish and Shellfish* section.

- Stretch seafood into salads, pastas, soups, stir-fries, and casseroles. A pound of grilled seafood can easily feed four to six people when it is combined with vegetables and starches, as in a stir-fry or chowder. Remember to do as the restaurants do: serve a half-pound of the expensive seafood (such as large shrimp or scallops) and use a less expensive filler (like cod) for the other half-pound. This will also allow you to share your divine seafood recipes with your guests without blowing your budget.

- Ask your retailer for frozen unthawed seafood. Ninety-five percent of shrimp and orange roughy comes into the United States frozen; there's no sense in purchasing thawed seafood and then refreezing it.

- The "grab-'n'-go" of the 1990's is carrying over into the new millennium, stronger than ever. However, eating out is expensive. Have seafood such as salmon, tuna, and shrimp in the freezer, so you can prepare a quick grilled salad or sandwich. Keep canned salmon and tuna on hand. Take 2 minutes before work to pour Italian salad dressing over your seafood and let it marinate in the refrigerator as it thaws during the day. Or, after work, quick-thaw frozen packaged seafood by running cool water over it for a few minutes. These ideas will help keep you from stopping at a restaurant on the way home when you are starving and want something fast.

- Preplan leftovers. After you have prepared your seafood dinner and satisfied everyone's appetite, cover and refrigerate the leftovers for later use. Restaurants pregrill chunks of seafood, shrimp, or scallops to add later to chowder. Doing the same will save you time and money!

Seafood Substitution Chart

Take this chart with you to the seafood counter. It will help you substitute familiar seafood with what's in season or on sale.

	Flavor		
Texture	**Mild** Very mild, bland	**Moderate** Balance of mellow and full flavor	**Full** Rich, bold, assertive
FIRM Big, meat- like flakes	Chilean sea bass Monkfish Tilefish Squid Tilapia Halibut Lingcod Kingklip Golden tilefish Grouper Hawaiian sea bass	Catfish, farmed Mahi-mahi Perch Swordfish Tuna, albacore Drum Octopus Clams Tuna	Salmon, sockeye, wild Salmon, king, wild Carp Shark Marlin

MEDIUM
Versatile,
medium flakes
and firmness
	Cod
	Crayfish
	Black sea bass
	Striped bass
	Sardines
	Oysters
	Sheepshead
	Sea trout
	Walleye pike
	Shrimp
	Black grouper
		Catfish, wild
		Tuna, albacore
		  canned
		Salmon, pink
		  wild, canned
		Mullet
		Shad
		Smelt
		Crab, imitation
		Salmon, chum, wild
		Orange roughy
		Snapper
		Sturgeon
			Salmon, sockeye
			  wild, canned
			Sardines, canned
			Mackerel
			Triggerfish
			Salmon, farmed

DELICATE Tender, soft, small flakes	Croaker Haddock Sole (flounder) Lake perch Pollock, Alaska Pomfret Scallops Spot Sculp (porgy)	Whiting (hake) Salmon, pink, wild Arctic char Crabmeat Buffalo fish Rainbow trout Skate	Bluefish Oysters Mussels, blue

At Home

Preparation Utensils

Good preparation utensils make a big difference and will save you time and energy.

- **Knives**
  - A thin, long, sharp knife for filleting
  - A heavy-duty knife for cutting through bone
  - A small knife for deveining and peeling shrimp
- **Pliers/tweezers**
  - For removing bones
- **Cutting board**
  - Two or three different sizes are recommended. We have several so we can do all our preparation on the different boards and then put all of them in the dishwasher to sanitize them.
- **Scaler**
  - You can purchase a scaler or simply use the back of a knife.

Forms of Fish

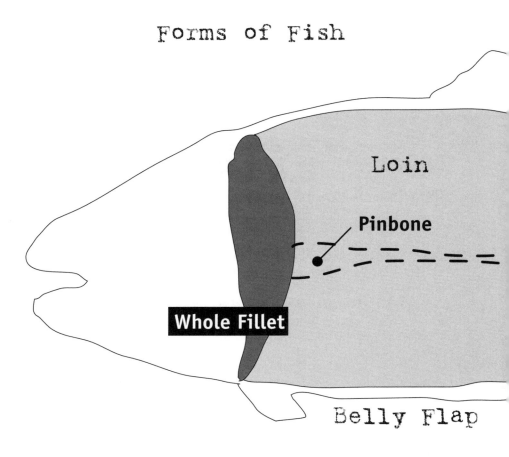

Loin

Pinbone

Whole Fillet

Belly Flap

The following forms of fish are usually the freshest and the most economical to grill. You can be a grill "showoff" to your friends and family by presenting them with an impressive whole grilled fish, but don't tell them how easy it is to prepare until they've slaved over doing the dishes!

WHOLE (LIVE)

This is straight from the waters, flippin' and kickin' all over your boat. The fish is still alive.

DRAWN

This form is how you would find a "whole" fish at a food market. It still looks like a whole fish, but it has been gutted. Any time you buy a drawn fish and cut it up yourself, you will save money.

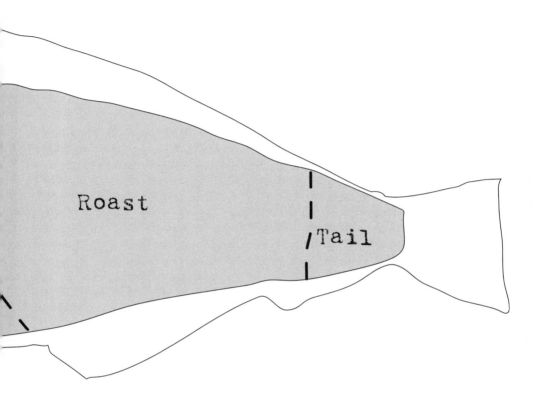

HEADED AND GUTTED, or H&G

Again, this fish is still in the form of a whole fish and has been gutted. In addition, the head, tail, and fins have been removed and the fish has usually been scaled.

FISH CUTS

You can purchase these precut at the fish market or catch or purchase a whole fish and chop it up yourself, using the diagrams on the following pages.

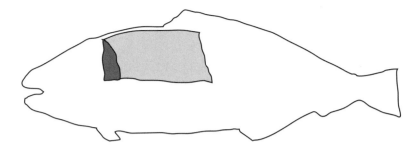

Loins

PRIME CUT: A red-meat lover's alternative. A loin cut is normally of uniform thickness, with no taper and no bones. Loins are taken from large fish—such as tuna, swordfish, or shark—and cut from the backbone lengthwise into quarters.

Grill Forms:
- Boneless/skinless

Grill Advantages:
- Prized cut
- Firm meat, easy to turn
- No waste

Grill Tricks:
- Chefs grill loins to an internal temperature of 120°F to keep meat moist and pink inside.

Grill Cuts:
- Versatile; can be cut into chunks for kabobs, tenders, or nuggets

FILLETING A ROUND FISH

*(See also **Filleting a Flat Fish**, page 34)*

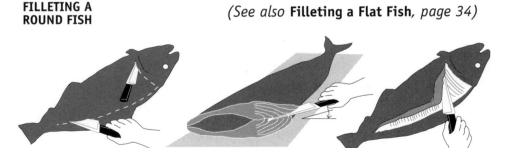

With fish facing away from you, use a sharp, thin-bladed knife. Cut along the back of fish from tail to head. Make a second cut just behind the gills, down to the backbone.

Holding the knife at a slight angle, cut along the bone to free the back side of the fillet.

Peel back the free meat, then cut fillet away from rib cage. Turn fish over and repeat previous steps for second fillet.

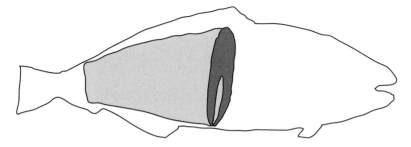

Roasts

CHOICE CENTER CUT: Roasts are taken from the tail end of fish (but do not include the tail), where the circumference of the fish is small and tapered. Roasts include the area of the belly that contains the most fat and provides fabulous moisture and flavor. Thickness varies with species.

Grill Forms: Bone in/skin on
  - Boneless/skin on: remove backbone; pull pinbones, but keep skin on
Grill Advantages:
  - Indirect heat/slow cook; great for entertaining
  - Fill body cavity with herbs, stuffing, or minced vegetables.
  - Loosely wrap fish to retain moisture. (Use banana leaves, foil, or the like.)
Grill Tricks: Turn fish with foil ropes. To make ropes:
  - Measure circumference of (distance around) fish, and use triple that length of foil
  - Twist aluminum foil lengthwise into a long rope. Repeat process for second rope.
  - Tie first rope around circumference of roast and twist foil tightly together to hold fish securely. Leave two long handles to make turning easy.
  - Repeat with second rope in the opposite direction.
  - Peel skin off after grilling and glaze with grill sauce.
Grill Cuts: Tied rolled roast: boneless and skinless; body cavity usually filled with stuffing. Tied with meat strings to hold it together.
Steaks/Fillets: Roast can be cut into steaks or fillets.

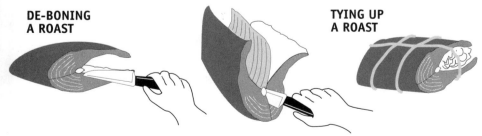

DE-BONING A ROAST

TYING UP A ROAST

With fish lying on its side, slide tip of knife between bone and meat starting at end. Slide knife down length of fish, cutting meat away from bone.

Hold fish on its back, cut from backbone to skin down length of fish, being careful not to cut skin. Repeat for other side. Pull out pinbones with tweezers.

Using heavy meat string, tie fish two or three times around circumference. Tie once or twice around length of roast.

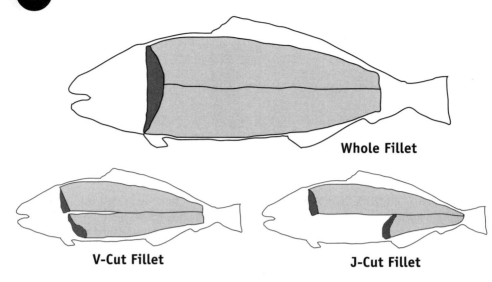

Whole Fillet

V-Cut Fillet

J-Cut Fillet

Fillets

Fillets are the sides of the fish cut away from the backbone and removed in one piece.

Grill Forms:
- Bone in/skin on
- Boneless/skin on
- Boneless/skinless

Grill Advantages:
- Beautiful presentation (lots of room for seared grill marks)
- Fillet tail cut will always be boneless.

Grill Tricks: Use foil or other barrier (skin) under fish.
- Grill fillets at least a half-inch thick.
- Place thin part of fillet (tail or belly) over cooler section of grill.
- Turn fish when it is undercooked but has grill marks on presentation side.

Grill Cuts:
- Versatile; can be cut into chunks for kabobs, tenders, or nuggets

**FILLETING A
FLAT FISH**
*(See also **Filleting a Round Fish,** page 32)*

With the eyed (dark) side of the flat fish up, use a flexible boning knife to make a cut along the spine from the gills to the tail.

Slide the blade between backbone and flesh, lifting fillet away from the bone. Remove the second fillet in the same manner. Turn fish over, repeat.

To skin, grasp fillet by the tail, skin side down. Holding the knife at a slight angle, cut the meat free.

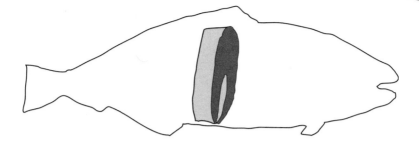

Steaks

Steaks are cross-sectional slices cut perpendicular to the backbone, usually 1 to 2 inches thick.

Grill Forms: Bone in/skin on; boneless/skinless

Grill Advantages: Uniform size for equal heat distribution and cooking time
- Meat-eater's alternative
- More economical than fillets
- Skin and bone give fuller flavor
- Easy to turn

Grill Tricks: Tuck belly flaps of steaks into body cavity during first 3 minutes of grilling. This will protect thin areas from overcooking.
- Bone and skin are easy to remove after steak is fully cooked. Use needlenose pliers to pull out backbone and pinbones. Remove skin by curling it around a fork tine.

Grill Cuts: Butterfly Cut:
- Remove backbone from steak.
- Keep skin on meat so steak is hinged.

Tenders/Strips:
- Remove backbone from steak.
- Remove skin.

Nuggets: Follow directions for tenders, but cut into smaller pieces.

**DEBONING & SKINNING
A STEAK**

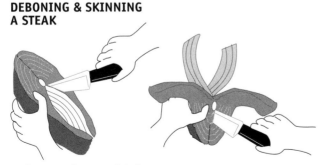

Cut bone away from meat in belly flaps. Repeat for other side.

Turn steak over, cut down from backbone to skin. To butterfly, do not cut through skin.

Slide knife under skin at belly flap. Cut meat away by moving knife up along steak until all skin is cut away.

CLEANING A CLAM

Wash thoroughly, discarding any that have broken shells or that do not close. Wearing a heavy glove, hold the clam in your palm and force the blade of a clam knIfe between the shells.

Run the knife around the edge of the shell to cut through the muscles holding it together.

Open clam and remove top shell. Use knife to loosen clam from bottom shell. Check for shell fragments before serving.

SHUCKING AN OYSTER

Wash oysters under cold running water and scrub with a stiff brush; discard those that are not tightly closed or that do not close quickly when handled. Place oyster, cupped side down, on a firm surface, holding it with gloved hand. Insert an oyster knife in the side opposite the hinge and twist.

Run the kinfe around the edge of the shell to cut the muscle that holds the two shells together.

Remove the top shell, and loosen oyster from bottom shell. Check for shell fragments before serving.

> **CLAMS, OYSTERS, & MUSSELS:** To grill, nestle open clams in rocksalt or crumpled foil. Top with sauces, salsas, or seasoned butters.

CLEANING A MUSSEL

 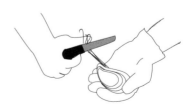

Prepare mussels as soon as possible after gathering. If mussels must be stored, refrigerate at 35°F. to 40°F. To prepare, scrub shells under cold, running water to remove grass and mud. Discard those that have open shells or shells that do not close quickly with handling.

Clip or pull beard; rinse mussel before cooking.

DRESSING A SOFT-SHELL CRAB

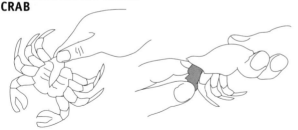

Remove the apron, the segmented abdominal part beneath the carapace (shell).

Lift the carapace's pointed ends, and remove spongy material.

Using scissors, cut about 1/2 inch behind the eyes and remove the face of the crab. What remains is the edible portion.

DRESSING A HARD-SHELL CRAB

Remove the apron, the segmented abdominal part beneath the carapace (shell).

Hold the back in one hand. Pry off the shell with the other hand.

Pull off and discard the spongy white gills from the body and tiny paddles from the front. Rinse the body well, then drain.

Pull the legs away from the body. Use a pliers or special crab pincers to crack open the leg segments. Remove meat with fingers or special crab pick.

Cut the body in two pieces down the middle (or break apart with hands).

To remove the meat from body, break apart along leg segments, removing meat with fingers or special crab pick.

PEELING & DEVEINING SHRIMP

 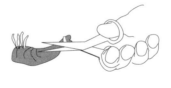 

Pull the head off where its armoring forms a natural division with the tail.

Peel off shell, leaving the legs, and cut lengthwise down the underside of the shrimp.

Pull the shell apart, removing the flesh.

 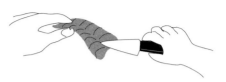

Using a tweezers or toothpick, remove the vein from the center of the back.

To butterfly, cut along the back of the shrimp, but not all the way through. Spread the halves open.

CLEANING A SQUID

Under cold, running water, rub off the dark, thin skin with your fingers.

Remove the one bony part from within the sac.

Use your fingers to push out the hard beak (mouth parts) hidden in the center of the tentacles and snip these away; cut away the eyes.

Hold the main sac firmly and pull all the tentacles together away from the sac. Be careful not to break the ink sac.

DRESSING A LOBSTER

For lobster that is to be grilled, rather than boiled live, cut off legs near body.

Insert a knife in the abdomen, and cut through the undershell toward the head, leaving the back shell intact.

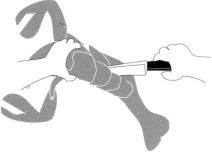

Cut toward the tail.

Press the lobster apart with your hands.

Remove the sand sac from the head; remove intestinal tract.

Chapter 4

At the Grill

At The Grill

Grilling Equipment

Grills

A variety of grills are available today at a variety of prices, from the small enclosure with bricks and a grill on top that you build yourself to the sophisticated new gas grills that might sing if you asked them to. Before you venture out into the "World Wide Web" of grills, think and talk about the kind of grill that will best suit your needs: indoor, outdoor, grill size (depending on the number of mouths you expect to be feeding), frequency of use, easily portable or stationary, cost, storage space, convenience, and cooking style. Because of the health benefits provided by grilling, we encourage year-round grilling, so we recommend having a grill that can be used outdoors when weather permits, as well as a grill that can be used inside when it doesn't.

INDOOR GRILLS

For indoor grilling, the number of grill types is more limited due to the constraints of indoor ventilation. Even grills designed for indoor use may set off the occasional smoke alarm when first searing the food, but opening windows and fanning the alarm with a dish towel should help turn it off!

There are four basic indoor grill options: ridged pans and griddles for stovetop use; broiler grilling pans (pans fitted with grates to be used under the broiler in the oven); electric tabletop grills (which can be used both indoors and outdoors); and grills built right into the kitchen.

OUTDOOR GRILLS

Outdoor grills offer a much greater selection. They can be divided into two categories: charcoal and gas/electric.

Charcoal

Uncovered grills, also called open grills, are generally the most basic and least expensive type of outdoor grill. They come in a variety of sizes, from portable tabletop grills to more elaborate models with added equipment (windscreens, half hoods, and so on). One of the more popular smaller versions of the uncovered charcoal grill is the hibachi. It is most commonly used, and ideal, for picnics and camping.

The difficulty with uncovered grills is that the food takes longer to cook because the heat is able to escape. In addition, the weather has a large influence on the quality of the grilled food by making it impossible to completely control the temperature inside the cooking chamber. The food also tends to taste less smoky (which may, in fact, make this type of grill desirable to some).

The covered grills (either kettle- or box-shaped) also come in a variety of sizes; they can be tabletop or standing models. When covered, these grills work much like an oven, reflecting heat off the lid onto all surfaces, thus cooking food more evenly and adding the ability to cook large, thick cuts of meat. (When uncovered, they perform just like an open grill.) Less heat is lost, so less charcoal is needed. The temperature of the grill is monitored more easily and controlled by dampers (regulating airflow) and adjustable grill heights. The dreaded flare-ups are minimal.

Food cooked in covered grills tends to have a deeper, richer smoky taste. The charcoal used in these grills requires some effort to ignite, preheats in approximately 30 minutes, and requires cleanup of the ashes when finished. Additional attachments are available, such as ash catchers and hinged cooking racks.

Charcoal Equipment

- Briquettes or charcoal: Avoid using self-lighting briquettes, as their aroma can overwhelm the delicate flavor of seafood; charcoal comes in a few different forms, so experiment to find your favorite.
- Tongs: These can be used to move hot briquettes or charcoal.
- Chimney starter, kindling, paraffin lighter cubes, or electric starter: Use one of these to get the coals going. Be careful when using lighter fluid, as it can leave lingering gassy tastes and unwanted additives. Be sure to give it enough time to burn off before adding your food to the grill.
- Butane lighter or other form of ignition: Unless you're using an electric starter, you'll need some kind of device that ignites the fire.

Gas and Electric Grills

Like the other types of grills, gas and electric grills are available in an assortment of sizes to accommodate your needs. These grills lead in convenience because of their no-hassle fire starter and no-mess cleanup. With the simple push of a button, the grill ignites and preheats in approximately 5 to 10 minutes. Temperature control is even easier on gas and electric grills, which have control knobs that regulate the amount of energy used. Electric grills are portable but do require a power outlet. Gas and electric grills are quite versatile, with many gadgets and options available: different sorts of burners, multilevel grills, work spaces, warmers, and more. You can get even more advanced with rotisserie grills and the like, but we will leave those for the chicken experts.

Included in this category is the pellet grill, which requires a power source and burns small wood pellets. While very efficient, it produces only indirect heat for cooking. It is a festive choice, as it comes in the shape of either a wild boar or a pig. It even spouts its smoke straight out of its nostrils. You won't need to call a clown for your party!

Gas Equipment

- Source of fuel: You'll need propane or natural gas.

Tools

Grilling experts all over the country agree on a few basic, universal tools that every grilling captain should have onboard. They will help make your grilling experience not only more enjoyable but also safer. A few of the items are fairly common, and you may already own some of them. The others can be purchased relatively inexpensively.

- **Long-handled tongs:** Used for lifting and turning foods.
- **Long-handled, extra-wide spatula:** Provides more surface space for lifting and turning.
- **Long-handled basting brushes:** Used for applying oil lightly on seafood to prevent sticking and for applying sauces.
- **Extra-long fireproof oven mitts:** Provide protection from hot tools/grill.

- **Brass grill brush:** After letting the grill burn on high heat to remove any food residue, clean off the grill rack with a brass brush. Brass bristles are softer than wire and will not scratch the grill rack.
- **Thermometer:** Instant-read tells you if you are too early, right on time, or too late.
- **Timer:** Helps keep track of cooking time, though grilling times are very approximate and are affected by many factors.
- **Sharp knife:** Makes for safe and easy cutting of food.
- **Skewers:** A variety of types are available (wood, metal, double-pronged or flat to prevent spinning, and even stripped rosemary).
- **Heavy-duty aluminum foil:** Many uses
- **Drip pan:** Used to catch food drippings; can be filled with a liquid (water, juice, broth, beer, wine) that evaporates and bastes the food automatically, keeping food moist and preventing drippings from burning; prevents flare-ups caused by drippings; can be as simple as a disposable aluminum pan or a pan lined with aluminum foil.

Favorite Tools and Techniques

Below we list some of our favorite tools and techniques. This list is intended to encourage you to become more experimental with your seafood grilling. No tool or technique is the "right" or "only" way to grill seafood. Whatever tools and techniques you choose will be the right way for you. Base your grilling techniques on what you have at home with regard to equipment, time, and desire. Sometimes the "same old way" is okay; other times, it's fun to put a new piece of grilling equipment on your wish list and hope "Santa" comes through.

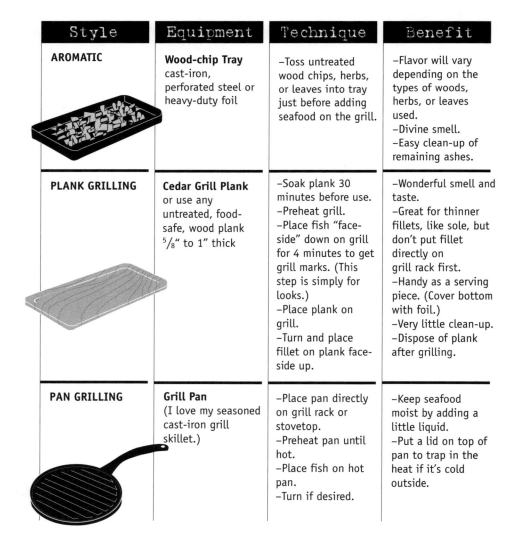

Style	Equipment	Technique	Benefit
AROMATIC	**Wood-chip Tray** cast-iron, perforated steel or heavy-duty foil	–Toss untreated wood chips, herbs, or leaves into tray just before adding seafood on the grill.	–Flavor will vary depending on the types of woods, herbs, or leaves used. –Divine smell. –Easy clean-up of remaining ashes.
PLANK GRILLING	**Cedar Grill Plank** or use any untreated, food-safe, wood plank $\frac{5}{8}$" to 1" thick	–Soak plank 30 minutes before use. –Preheat grill. –Place fish "face-side" down on grill for 4 minutes to get grill marks. (This step is simply for looks.) –Place plank on grill. –Turn and place fillet on plank face-side up.	–Wonderful smell and taste. –Great for thinner fillets, like sole, but don't put fillet directly on grill rack first. –Handy as a serving piece. (Cover bottom with foil.) –Very little clean-up. –Dispose of plank after grilling.
PAN GRILLING	**Grill Pan** (I love my seasoned cast-iron grill skillet.)	–Place pan directly on grill rack or stovetop. –Preheat pan until hot. –Place fish on hot pan. –Turn if desired.	–Keep seafood moist by adding a little liquid. –Put a lid on top of pan to trap in the heat if it's cold outside.

Style	Equipment	Technique	Benefit
PACKET GRILLING	Heavy-duty aluminum foil	–Cut foil to size of seafood, allowing for folding top and ends. –Wrap seafood loosely, leaving a steam hole in foil. –Insert temperature probe through steam hole in foil.	–Simple. –Pile full of vegetables to make a one-packet meal. –Holds smaller and fine-texture seafood together. –Make ahead and refrigerate. –Little clean-up. –Easy to transport. (Keep in cooler until placed on grill.) –Eat right out of packet.
WIRE BASKET GRILLING	Hinged or unhinged wire basket	–Oil basket before putting in seafood. –Lay seafood inside basket. Make sure basket is closed tight before placing on grill. –Turn basket half-way through grilling.	–Easy to lift and turn whole fish. –Prevents squid and lobster tails from curling. –Keeps small seafood such as shrimp, clams, and mussels in shell from falling through.
FINE WIRE MESH RACK	Fine wire mesh rack For our wedding we used chicken wire. Cookie cooling racks and fine wire screens work, too.	–Lay seafood on oiled grill. –Turn fish if you want grill marks, if not, cover with foil to trap in heat and smoke.	–Provides a surface on which to grill small seafood.

Grilling Style

Now that you have chosen the type of grill that is best for you, you need to learn how to use it. We will cover several different types of grilling methods over the next few pages. Once again, we recommend that you try them and discover for yourself which style produces the results that are most scrumptious to you and your family. We are confident that you will find just the flavor you are looking for!

Direct

Direct grilling, sometimes also called fast cooking, calls for the food to be placed directly over the heat source. The grill can be either covered or uncovered, but if the temperature outside is cool, you may want to close the lid after the food is turned in order to keep the grilled side of the food warm. Due to the intense heat, more browning tends to occur on the outside of the food. Most seafood is cooked by this method, which is usually used for foods that require less than 25 minutes to cook. Depending on its thickness, the fish is usually turned once halfway through the cooking time. (For thin fillets, you need not bother.)

Direct grilling

To grill by the direct method on a charcoal grill:
- Evenly distribute the hot coals across the charcoal grate. Place the food in the center of the preheated cooking grill. (Refer to the following section, *Grilling Procedures*.)

To grill by the direct method on a gas or electric grill:
- Place the food in the center of the preheated cooking grate, directly above the burners. (Refer to the following section, *Grilling Procedures*.)

Indirect

Indirect grilling, or slow grilling, cooks the food away from direct contact with the heat source. This technique is used for thicker, larger foods that need more cooking time. The grill must stay covered in order to keep the temperature constant inside. That means no peeking! With the lid down, less oxygen enters, keeping the heat lower. (Be sure the vents are open so that the fire is not smothered due to lack of oxygen.) Much as in a convection oven, the heat circulates, reflecting off the sides and lid. The food cooks slowly and evenly and does not

Indirect grilling

require turning. A drip pan is placed beneath the food and can be filled with water or a desired liquid (juice, broth, beer, wine) to help the food retain its moisture and to keep the drippings from burning. Make sure this liquid does not dry up; depending on your grilling time, you may need to refill the drip pan several times throughout the cooking period.

To grill by the indirect method on a charcoal grill:
- Arrange the hot coals on the sides of the grill, leaving the middle area free from coals.
- Place the drip pan between the coals.
- With the grill rack back on, put your food directly above the drip pan, so that now the coals are off to the sides of the food.

To grill by the indirect method on a gas or electric grill:
- Turn the preheated burner off beneath where the food will be set.
- Place the drip pan above the "off" burner and below where the food is set.
- Place the food on the grill rack and adjust the burner(s) on the side of the food to the desired temperature.

Covered

As discussed earlier in the *Grilling Equipment* section, the grilling captain has the choice of grilling with the lid on or off. Some grilling experts say always cook with the lid down, and some say never. We say try them both; there is no right or wrong, but these two methods do provide significantly different and distinct flavors. Learn by trying!

When using the covered technique, place food on the grill rack. Lower the lid to completely cover the grill. (Note: If you do not have a lid, simply make a tent type of lid out of heavy-duty aluminum foil.) Resist the temptation to keep looking at your perfectly grilling food; every time you open the grill, the heat escapes, adding time to your cooking clock and growls to your tummy. There is no peeking allowed while grilling covered style! An electronic thermometer on a long wire and metal probe can be inserted into the seafood while a data box, reading both the temperature of the grill surface and the internal temperature, can be placed outside the grill and monitored during grilling. (Once again, remember to keep your grill vents open to provide enough oxygen to keep your fire going!)

If you cover your grill during cooking, your food will have a much deeper and richer smoky flavor than food cooked on an uncovered grill. If you have added any other aromatic enhancers (wood chips, herbs, or the like), you will also find these flavors to be strongly cooked into your foods. Covered grills work much like ovens, circulating the heat inside to evenly cook the food at a lower temperature. This type of cooking environment is easier to control and monitor. Flare-ups are minimal, reducing the chance of charring the outside of your meat and leaving the inside raw. Do remember that a covered grill is required if you are grilling by the indirect cooking method.

Uncovered

The uncovered technique obviously means that you leave the grill lid off and the food exposed after placing it on the preheated rack. Uncovering your grill during cooking increases the amount of oxygen inside, making the coals burn hotter. On the other hand, large quantities of heat easily escape, and the wind and air temperature outside will alter your cooking time and temperature. Often used for small, thin foods, the open grill quickly sears in the juices, crisping the outside and trapping the flavor inside. The grilled food generally has a less smoky flavor.

Dry

Grilling is a form of dry heat cooking. Dry heat cooking is a little tricky and requires single-minded attention. You will need to follow the time, temperature, and texture rules closely, as explained in the following section, *Grilling Procedures*. Check the fish before you expect it to be done; it is better to be too early than too late! Most fish and shellfish grilling times will be short, and controls against drying out must be stringent because fish and seafood have little internal fat. If you are a first-time seafood griller, you may wish to start learning on a higher-fat fish, such as salmon, mackerel, or catfish.

Moist

Various techniques can be used to provide moist heat during grilling. Drip pans are an effective means of replenishing moisture. Place a disposable aluminum pan beneath your food and partially fill it with the liquid of your choice: water, juice, broth, wine, or beer. Also try basting your seafood or "wrapping" your fish. These techniques are described in the *Grilling Techniques* section later in this chapter.

Adding moisture with a drip pan

Broiling

Broiling is different from grilling in that the food is placed beneath the heat source as opposed to above it. The broiling coil on the underside of your oven (or the gas flame broiler if you have a gas stove) cooks the food placed beneath it on a broiler grilling pan, a shallow pan fitted with a slatted grate. The bottom pan serves as a drip pan and can be filled with a liquid (water, juice, broth, beer, wine) to provide steam basting and prevent any food drippings from burning. The top pan has a look and effect somewhat like that of a grill rack. The slits allow the drippings to run off the food and fall to the pan below.

- Turn your oven to the broiler setting.
- Preheat your broiler grilling pan.
- Place your food on the preheated broiler grilling pan.

- Place your broiler grilling pan in the oven. Fish should be approximately 3 to 4 inches from the heat source.
- Seafood should be turned once halfway through grilling time, unless it is very thin (a half-inch or less), in which case turning is not necessary.

Grilling Procedures

Before considering specific methods, it's important to go over some universal rules that make for great grilling. Again . . . *read carefully all of the manufacturer's instructions that came with your grilling unit.* They will teach you not only how to manage your grill safely, but also how to maximize its use. We make suggestions in this book with regard to grilling safety and procedures, but the ultimate authority is the manufacturer. Never do anything that does not comply with the recommendations for your grill.

Preheating

Preheating is a very important part of grilling. Regardless of the kind of food or type of grill, preheating the grill makes for attractive and easier cooking. First, preheating allows you to get those great seared marks on your food. Second, since food has a tendency to stick to cold surfaces, a preheated grill rack helps to prevent the food from latching onto those bars.

Using a chimney to start coals

To preheat a charcoal grill:
- Pile the coals in a heap in the center of the grill.
- Light the coals using your choice of ignition (chimney starter, electric starter, paraffin lighter cubes).
- Allow the coals to burn for approximately 30 minutes, or until they are covered in a light-gray ash and are no longer flaming.

To preheat a gas or electric grill:
- Be sure to refer to your instructions on how to start your grill; directions may vary slightly.
- Once the grill is burning, close the lid and let all the burners burn on high for 10 minutes. The grill should heat to approximately 500°F.

To preheat grilling pans:
- Place broiler grilling pans in a heated oven for 10 minutes; place stovetop grilling pans/griddles on a burner for 10 minutes.

Grill Temperature Test

You can control the temperature of the grill to some extent by the amount of fuel you supply and the oxygen you allow in through the vents. In this book, we use terms such as "medium" or "high" to describe the temperature needed for certain types of foods, as detailed in the chart below.

450°F and above	High
375°–450°F	Medium-High
325°–375°F	Medium
250°–325°F	Medium-Low
250°F and below	Low

If your grill does not come with an internal thermometer that reads the grill surface, you can purchase an oven or grill thermometer. Or purchase one that is portable and can be used to tell both the surface grill temperature and the internal temperature of the seafood.

Briquette manufacturers recommend approximately 25 to 30 briquettes to hold a fire for 45 minutes on a grill that is 22$\frac{1}{2}$ inches in diameter. That number of briquettes will reach a grill temperature of approximately 350°F. Add eight more briquettes every 45 minutes to hold the temperature.

Time, Temperature, and Texture

Overcooking and drying out one's seafood meal is one of the griller's biggest fears. Most seafood grilling techniques use dry heat, so the flesh is losing its natural moisture all the time it's grilling. (Fish meat is 70 percent water.) The higher the internal cooking temperature of your fish, the more natural moisture is removed from it. As the internal cooking temperature increases, the flesh begins to turn firm and opaque. You can learn how cooked fish feels by sticking the point of a sharp knife into the layers of connective tissue (myocommata). As this tissue cooks, it turns to gelatin and melts away. That is why fish flakes when cooked. As you become accustomed to using time, temperature, and texture as a grilling gauge, you can determine how you like your seafood cooked, from rare to well done.

Grilling temperature and time are affected by a number of variables, only some of which are under your control. The wind, humidity, air temperature, and temperature of the uncooked fish will influence the grill temperature and alter the time needed for cooking. Use a combination of time, temperature, and texture to determine when your fish is cooked. Grilling is not a science, and cooking times are approximate and subject to personal preference. Use the following suggestions as guidelines, but do check food frequently, as it is better to be too early than too late!

Time

The Canadian Department of Fisheries and Oceans recommends that fish be cooked 10 minutes per inch of thickness, measuring at the thickest part of the fish.

**MEASURING
A FILLET**

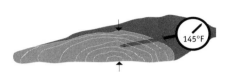

Measure fillet at thickest point. Cook 10 minutes per inch of thickness. To use thermometer, insert through side of fillet at thickest point.

**MEASURING
A ROAST**

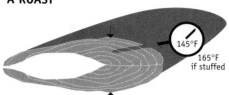

Measure roast at thickest point. Cook 10 minutes per inch of thickness. To use thermometer, insert through side of roast at thickest point.

Hint: Strategically plan your menu, working backward. Foods with the longest cooking time go on the grill first; foods with the shortest cooking time go last. Oysters in the shell are great appetizers and can be grilled before your guests arrive. They will be sure to entertain your guests while the main course is on the grill.

Temperature

The FDA recommends grilling fish until its internal temperature reaches 145°F. Most chefs use a range of internal cooking temperatures, from 120° to 145°F, and pull their fish off the grill a few seconds shy of its fully cooked time or temperature. Fish will continue to cook after it's removed from the grill, so this allows the fish to keep cooking but not overcook.

Using Two Temperatures for Maximum Results

Different parts of the grill rack will vary in heat intensity, making the rack ideal for cooking a variety of fillet thicknesses and seafood shapes. Usually the fillet tail section is thinner than the body. Place the thinner section over the least intense heat. You can move the thin tail section to a "hot spot" to finish cooking if needed. Similarly, varying steak thicknesses can be grilled at the same time by placing the thinner steaks over the least intense heat.

Texture

Another way of checking for doneness is to see and feel when your fish is cooked. The cooking changes are most pronounced and easiest to read using this method. It takes a little practice, though, so start learning it on a salmon fillet or steak.

See: As bright-red (raw) king salmon meat is grilled, it will turn orange-red (cooked). Check the interior of the fish a few minutes before you expect it to be done. Use a thin-blade knife to peek between the layers of flesh. When it's cooked, your knife should meet no resistance. Generally the flesh is no longer transparent but rather opaque.

Feel: Press lightly with your spatula on the salmon fillet. Through experience, you can learn to distinguish the feel of cooked fish (firm) from raw meat (bouncy). Note that tuna, swordfish, marlin, and shark are all exceptions: when raw, their meat is naturally firm, so monitoring their internal temperature with a thermometer is very important when grilling them.

Time and Temperature Chart

	Weight or Thickness	Grill Heat	Grill Time	Grilling Method	Doneness Test and Appearance
FILLETS, STEAKS, AND SEAFOOD KABOBS					
Fillets and steaks	$1/_2$ inch	Med.-High	6-8 min.	direct	Turn from moist, translucent color to opaque; flake when tested with fork; firm to touch
Kabobs	1 inch	Med.-High	3-5 min.	direct	(See specific species)
WHOLE AND STUFFED FISH					
Fish, whole	1 inch	Medium	10-12 min.	indirect	Test internal temp. with thermometer (145°F)
Fish, whole stuffed	2 inch	Medium	20-25 min.	indirect	Test internal temp. with thermometer (165°F)
SHELLFISH					
Clams, shell on	6 medium	Med.-High	5-7 min.	direct	Pop open
Crab, whole	$\sim 2^1/_2$ lbs.	Medium	10-12 min.	direct	Turns bright orange
Lobster, whole	~ 2 lbs.	Medium	18-20 min.	direct	Turns bright orange
Lobster, tails	8-10 oz.	Medium	8-10 min.	direct	Turn bright orange
Mussels, shell on	6 medium	Med.-High	5-7 min.	direct	Pop open
Oysters, shell on	6 medium	Med.-High	7-12 min.	direct	Pop open, meat edges curl and firm slightly
Scallops, shell off	6 medium	Medium	2-3 min.	direct	Turn from moist, translucent color to opaque
Shrimp, shell on	6 large	High	5-7 min.	direct	Turn bright orange
Shrimp, shell off	6 large	High	2-3 min.	direct	Turn pink and opaque
Squid strips	$1/_4$ inch wide	Med.-High	1-2 min.	direct	Hot to touch

Oiling the Food

Nothing is worse than a perfectly grilled fish that you can't get off the grill. Because stuck-on foods are no fun, we highly recommend that you lightly brush or spray vegetable oil on the food itself before laying it on the grill. Excess oil will drip off during cooking—but remember, oil drippings cause flare-ups, so don't overdo it!

Cleaning the Grill

You could do everything else right, but if you put your food on a dirty grill, you may never get it off again. Always begin with a clean grill, or should I say, always *end* with a clean grill.

- After you have finished cooking, remove your meal from the grill and close the lid (if you have one). Turn all the burners on high or leave the coals to continue burning. Let the heat burn off any food or oil residue. This may take up to 15 minutes.
- Afterward, use your brass brush to scrub the rack while it is still hot, breaking off any remaining residue. You do not want to apply too much pressure; you just want to remove any chunks of food or burnt sauce drippings.
- Do not let ashes accumulate in a charcoal grill or let residue collect in a gas grill. The cleaner you keep your grill, the less chance there is of it harboring anything that might alter the flavor of your food.

Storing the Grill

When you are not busy grilling up a salmon steak, keep your grill well protected and store it beneath a waterproof cover. Ideally, store the grill in a covered structure, such as a bike shed, garage, or storage shed. This will help prolong the life of your grill.

Grilling Techniques

Searing/Branding

For visual appeal, you can create attractive grill marks by branding them into your food. The intense heat immediately sears the food with authentic grill marks. Besides producing marks that look great, searing enhances the flavor by sealing in the juices. Following the completion of your searing, finish cooking by using the grilling method that you have chosen. Searing does not cook the inside of your food; it simply makes it more visually enticing. For greatest effectiveness, change the location of the food when turning it, and place it on a part of the grill that has not yet been used to sear food. Unused parts of the grill will be sizzling hot and produce great marks!

SEARING/BRANDING

With a paper towel, pat off excess moisture.

Place food directly over heat source. Cook 1-2 minutes. Repeat for marks on both sides.

For cross-hatch look, rotate food 45 degrees before flipping food over to get a second set of marks.

- Preheat your grill.
- With a paper towel, pat off any excess moisture on the food to help promote maximum browning and searing.
- Place the food directly over the heat source on the hot grill rack. Keeping the lid down (if you have one) on your grill during searing will keep the grill hotter and more effective for searing.
- Cook for 1 to 2 minutes. If you want marks on both sides, flip your food over and repeat the process.

To get the cross-hatch look:
- Following the steps above, sear the first set of lines.
- Rotate your food about 45 degrees and sear a second set of lines.

Oils

The smoking point of oil is important to know when grilling. The higher the smoking point, the better suited the oil is for grilling. We use extra-light olive oil with a smoking point of 470°F for coating fish and shellfish to prevent them from sticking on the grill. Other oils with a high smoking point are corn, canola, peanut, and sunflower.

Marinating

Marinating your seafood before grilling helps it retain a little extra moisture, and at the same time enhances its delicate flavor. Marinades should not overwhelm the seafood's taste but rather complement it. We recommend that you marinate your fish for no more than 30 minutes. Marinating it for too long will actually begin to "cook" the fish, as in ceviche. For marinating tips, refer to Chapter 11, *Marinades, Rubs, and Basting Sauces.*

Hint: Look for reduced-sodium broth, soy sauces, and other condiments to get the great taste without all the extra salt.

Basting

Basting helps to keep seafood moist during grilling. In the previous section, we discussed the use of a drip pan as a means of keeping fish moist. Another version of the drip pan, which works for any type of seafood, is referred to as "the boat." Tear off a piece of aluminum foil several inches longer than your fish. On a flat surface, fold each of the four sides up to build a 1-inch "wall." Fold the wall over a couple of times to secure its strength. You should now have a flat-bottomed boat to lay your fish in and partially fill with basting liquid. With this method, you do not have to worry about drippings causing flare-ups.

You can also baste your food by using your long-handled basting brush. Carefully cover the top of your seafood with your favorite sauce. Be aware that if your sauce contains oils or fat, the drippings will cause flare-ups. Do not overdo it. Be aware of the types of ingredients you are using in your sauce and how grill-friendly they are. For example, many commercial barbecue sauces are made with tomatoes and sugar, both of which burn very easily at low temperatures. Brush on thick or sweet sauces during the last minutes of grilling time or after the grill has been turned off.

Wrapping

Wrapping uncooked fish and shellfish is a fun grilling technique that retains the seafood's internal and natural liquids. Try wrapping your seafood meal in individual packets of cornhusks or grape, banana, or lettuce leaves. This makes for a dramatic presentation right off the grill! Aluminum foil will work, too; however, by completely covering the food in foil, you will block out much of the flavorful effect of grilling.

Skewers

Soaking your wood skewers in water for approximately 30 minutes will help to prevent them from charring and becoming fragile. Or add a little more flavor to your kabob pieces by soaking the skewers in cider, wine, port, bourbon, or sherry instead of water.

Dry or Wet Spice Rubs

The herb world is at your fingertips. Crushed, chopped, minced, dried, and fresh herbs all make wonderful rubs.

- Dry seafood with a paper towel. (The rub will stick better and be more evenly coated when seafood is dry.)
- Sprinkle or spread seafood with the desired amount of rub.
- Rub-a, rub-a, rub-a onto your seafood.
- Let sit for 5 minutes.
- Lightly spray with vegetable cooking oil.
- Place on the grill. It's just that simple.

Tricks to Turning

Turning fish can be a disaster, but it does not need to be. Here are a variety of tricks and tips to get your fish to flip to the other fin. Honest, you will soon be flipping your fragile-falling-fish blues away!

Turning your fish is not always required, but we do recommend it when the thickness exceeds a half-inch (unless otherwise noted—for instance, you do not need to turn a fish being cooked on a plank). We recommend turning for two main reasons: it cooks the food more evenly as well as succulently flavoring both sides with the highly prized grill taste, and it shows off the grill marks you have expertly seared on both sides.

Fish

- Some tools mentioned earlier in this chapter are made specifically for the purpose of turning ease, such as the wire grilling basket (especially excellent for whole fish).
- You can use a grill rack with grates that are closer together to eliminate large gaps.
- Leaving the skin on your fish cuts is helpful in holding the meat together.
- Fish fillets usually seem to put up the biggest fight and cause the most problems. We have found success in first placing the fillet meat-side down (presentation side) for approximately 2 minutes, allowing the intense heat to quickly sear the fish and just start to penetrate the meat. Then, with your large spatula (use two if it helps), gently flip your fillet over so the skin side is down. Now you have successfully turned your fish before it cooks through and gets to the delicate flaky stage!

Shellfish

- All shellfish are very low in fat and will overcook quickly. Turn large shellfish after just a minute on the grill. Then, to retain moisture, baste with your favorite marinade while the shellfish finishes grilling.
- Use tongs to turn shellfish. Tongs will not pierce the shellfish, which would cause it to lose precious moisture. They will also give you a better grip on the meat, making it less likely that it will fall through the grill rack.
- Don't turn oysters in the shell, but do note this important fact: Oysters in

the shell have two sides, a lid that is flat and a cup that is bowl-shaped. To make sure the natural juices in the oysters are retained, be sure to place them on the grill with the lid side up.

Aromatic Grilling

There are a variety of objects you can use during grilling to add to the flavor and scent of your meal, thus enhancing the grilling experience. This aromatic adventure provides a healthy way to prepare and flavor your meal without adding any extra calories or fat. Sniffing sage steaming through your scallops or cedar soaking into your salmon steaks will make you salivate and scream for satisfaction!

Wood
(Chips, Chunks, and Tree Cuttings)

For centuries, French winemakers have taken their grapevine trimmings and tossed them into the burning fire because of the flavor they impart to food. Burning wood trimmings while grilling adds a smoky-woodsy flavor. You can seek out trimmings in the forest beyond the yard, or you can "dot-com it" and order them off the Internet.

Wood comes in an assortment of sizes, flavors, and types. Chips are ideal for backyard grills, where the space between the heat source and the grate is close. Chunks are ideal for very large grills and for long, slow grilling. Soak the wood in water (or the liquid of your choice) for 30 to 60 minutes. Drain the wood thoroughly and then toss it into the grill just before placing the food on the rack. Remember, putting the grill lid down will concentrate the smoke and create a stronger flavor. If you have any fruit trees, try tossing on some of the twigs.

Here are some of the woods that are recommended to complement seafood, especially fish. Be careful with mesquite, as the flavor can become strong very quickly. You may want to leave the lid off for that one!

	FLAVOR
Alder	Hint of sweetness
Apple	Sweet and mildly fruity
Ash	Light but distinctive
Beechwood	Woodsy taste
Cherry	Mildly fruity
Mesquite	Rich, earthy flavor
Oak	Lighter version of mesquite
Pecan	Fruity

Herbs

Herbs, too, can impart extra delicate flavor to your food. Fresh herbs are always ideal, but dried herbs will also do the trick—just add a little extra. Soak the herbs in water for at least 30 minutes beforehand, and then sprinkle them over the hot grill just before adding your food. Use herbs that will complement your food and ingredients. Give some of these a try with your seafood: thyme, rosemary, dill, basil, oregano, bay leaves, marjoram, and sage.

Nutshells

Try lightly cracking some of your favorite nuts, such as almonds, pecans, or walnuts. Soak the shells in water for 20 minutes and then toss them on the hot grill just before putting your food on the grill rack. Save your nutshells from the family holiday gatherings!

Leaves

Throwing onto the grill a few wet leaves from trees such as maple, alder, oak, hickory, or fruitwoods (especially apple) will add lots of smoke and flavor. Just be sure that your leaves are suitable for cooking and come from unsprayed trees.

Seaweed and Kelp

Want more of a "sea" taste? Haul a pocketful of seaweed or kelp home from the beach and toss it on the grill. If it's dried, soak it in water before adding it to the grill. You will almost hear the waves crashing and seagulls cawing!

Planks

This classic, ancient technique is adopted from the Native Americans, who split open their freshly caught salmon, tied it to a piece of driftwood, and cooked it standing vertically downwind of a blazing fire. Be aware that a great amount of smoke will be produced, but this is what you want. It is this delicious smoke that in effect will "cook" the food.

You can employ this technique on your grill easily enough. Numerous companies make ready-to-use planks specifically for this purpose. Otherwise, you can trot on down to your local lumberyard and make one yourself. Be *very* sure that the wood you purchase is *un*treated! It should be no more than 1 inch thick ($^5/_8$ inch is recommended), 8 to 10 inches wide, and (depending on the length of your fish) 10 to 12 inches long. Ask the store to cut the lengths of the boards for you.

Two of the most popular types of planking wood are cedar and alderwood. Other recommended types include maple, oak, hickory, peach, and applewood. Before using the plank, soak it in water for a minimum of 30 minutes—overnight works well, too. Weigh it down with a heavy rock or can to completely submerge it in the water. You don't need to oil the plank before positioning the food on it. Place the plank with fish directly over the heat source and close the lid. You will not need to turn the fish. Do not yield to the temptation to peek at your food; both the smoke and heat will escape the cooking chamber. Plank cooking requires a constant level of high heat for the entire cooking time. Keep your grill well stocked with fuel! Keep a spray bottle of water on hand, as you may need to extinguish sparks that begin igniting on the plank. Do not let the plank dry out; it is wood and can ignite.

With a slight variation, planking also works in a conventional oven. Lay the plank in a roasting pan and pour in the liquid you want to flavor the food with, partially filling the pan. Preheat in a very hot oven for about 5 minutes. Place the fish on the plank. This method cooks the food using aromatic steam. Presoaking the plank in water is not necessary in this case, because the plank is submerged in liquid during cooking, but do keep an eye on the level of the liquid, as it will evaporate. Replenish as necessary. Now carry your prize-winning planked salmon fillet to the center of your table. The dramatic presentation is sure to receive "oohs" and "aahs" from all of your guests!

You may sometimes prefer a surface that cooks very quickly and evenly but does not impart flavor. Stone surfaces such as terra-cotta, marble, or granite work great. You can also purchase ceramic baking stones that are intended for that purpose. Just imagine serving your freshly grilled fish on something as captivating as marble!

Chapter 5
Kabobs

Albacore Tuna
with Cilantro-Basil Rub

1 lb. tuna, cut into 1″ chunks

SERVES: 4   **SUBSTITUTIONS: shark, shrimp**

CILANTRO-BASIL RUB

3 garlic cloves, minced

3 T. red chili paste

2 T. fresh cilantro, minced

2 T. fresh basil, minced

1 T. fresh ginger, grated

1 tsp. olive oil

1 tsp. light soy sauce

Mix all Cilantro-Basil Rub ingredients in large glass dish.

Place tuna in dish and coat with Cilantro-Basil Rub. Cover and marinate in refrigerator for 15 minutes.

Remove tuna from marinade. Thread tuna on skewers.

Place skewers on grill for 2 minutes. Turn. Grill for approximately 2 more minutes.

Calculations per Serving:
153 calories
2 gm total fat
0 gm saturated fat
51 mg cholesterol
326 mg sodium

Heat Source: Direct   **Temp:** Medium-High

Diabetic Exchanges:
3 meat

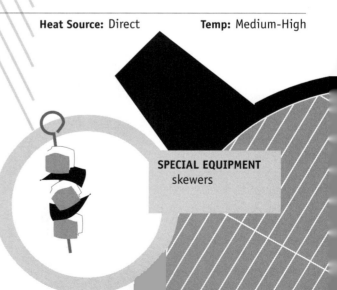

SPECIAL EQUIPMENT
skewers

Canadian Bacon & Scallop Kabobs

1 lb. sea scallops
1 C. Teriyaki Dipping Sauce *(see Chapter 11)*
¹/₄ lb. Canadian bacon, cut in half
vegetable oil

SERVES: 4   **SUBSTITUTIONS:** salmon, swordfish, halibut

Combine scallops and Teriyaki Dipping
    Sauce in medium glass dish. Cover
    and marinate in refrigerator for 15
    minutes.
Remove scallops from marinade. Wrap a
    piece of Canadian bacon around each
    scallop and thread on skewers.
Using basting brush, lightly coat kabobs
    with vegetable oil. Place on grill for 2
    minutes. Turn.
Grill for approximately 3 more minutes.

Temp: Medium-High   **Heat Source:** Direct

Calculations per Serving:
156 calories
3 gm total fat
1 gm saturated fat
53 mg cholesterol
884 mg sodium

Diabetic Exchanges:
¹/₂ fruit
3 meat

SPECIAL EQUIPMENT
    skewers
    basting brush

Curried Shark Satay

1 lb. shark, boneless, skinless, cut into $\frac{1}{2}$"-wide, 3"-long strips
vegetable oil

SERVES: 4

SUBSTITUTIONS: swordfish, shrimp, tilefish

MARINADE

1 C. plain low-fat yogurt
2 T. orange juice
2 T. curry powder
$\frac{1}{4}$ tsp. ground ginger
$\frac{1}{4}$ tsp. salt

Mix all marinade ingredients in a Ziploc™ bag. Blend well.

Add shark strips to bag. Seal and marinate in refrigerator for 15 minutes.

Remove shark from marinade. Thread fish on skewers in an "S" shape.

Using basting brush, lightly coat satays with vegetable oil. Place on grill for 2 minutes. Turn.

Grill for approximately 2 more minutes.

Calculations per Serving:
175 calories
7 gm total fat
1 gm saturated fat
57 mg cholesterol
136 mg sodium

Heat Source: Direct   **Temp:** Medium-High

Diabetic Exchanges:
3 meat

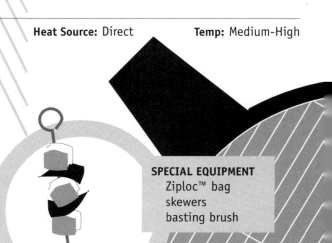

SPECIAL EQUIPMENT
Ziploc™ bag
skewers
basting brush

Easy Seafood Brochettes

1 lb. mixed seafood, such as large peeled shrimp, scallops, and 1" fish chunks
1 C. light Italian salad dressing
vegetable oil

SERVES: 4   **SUBSTITUTIONS: oysters, tuna, monkfish**

Place all seafood in large glass dish.
Pour Italian salad dressing over seafood.
    Cover and marinate in refrigerator for
    15 minutes.
Remove seafood from marinade. Thread
    seafood on skewers.
Using basting brush, lightly coat
    brochettes with vegetable oil. Place
    on grill for 2 minutes. Turn.
Grill for approximately 2 more minutes.

Temp: Medium-High   **Heat Source:** Direct

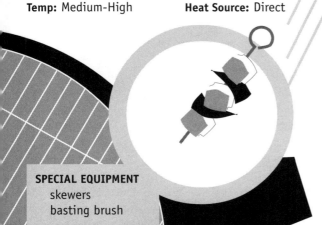

Calculations per Serving:
129 calories
3 gm total fat
0 gm saturated fat
82 mg cholesterol
282 mg sodium

Diabetic Exchanges:
3 meat

SPECIAL EQUIPMENT
skewers
basting brush

Hawaiian Kabobs

1 lb. tuna, boneless, skinless, cut into 1" chunks
1 20-oz. can pineapple chunks, drained (reserve ¹/₄ C. juice)
vegetable cooking spray

SERVES: 6

SUBSTITUTIONS: swordfish, marlin, salmon

MARINADE

¹/₄ C. reserved
   pineapple juice
2 T. light soy sauce
2 T. sherry
2 T. olive oil
1 tsp. brown sugar
1 tsp. ground ginger
¹/₂ tsp. dry mustard
¹/₄ tsp. lemon-pepper
   seasoning

Mix all marinade ingredients in small
   saucepan. Bring to a boil.
Reduce heat and simmer uncovered for 5
   minutes. Cool.
Pour marinade into Ziploc™ bag and add
   tuna chunks. Seal and marinate in
   refrigerator for 15 minutes.
Remove tuna from marinade. Alternate
   pineapple and fish on skewers.
Lightly coat kabobs with vegetable spray.
   Place on grill for 2 minutes. Turn.
Grill for approximately 2 more minutes.

Calculations per Serving:
157 calories
3 gm total fat
0 gm saturated fat
34 mg cholesterol
110 mg sodium

Heat Source: Direct   **Temp:** Medium-High

Diabetic Exchanges:
1 fruit
2¹/₂ meat

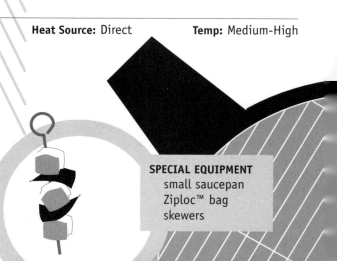

SPECIAL EQUIPMENT
small saucepan
Ziploc™ bag
skewers

Moroccan Halibut Kabobs

1 lb. halibut, boneless, skinless, cut into 1" chunks
1 medium red bell pepper, seeded, cut into 1" pieces
1 medium sweet onion, cut into 1" pieces
vegetable oil

SERVES: 4   **SUBSTITUTIONS: lobster, triggerfish**

Microwave bell pepper and onion in covered microwave dish for 2 minutes.

Combine all seasoning ingredients in large bowl.

Add halibut and vegetables to seasoning and toss to coat evenly.

Thread on skewers, alternating halibut and vegetables.

Using basting brush, lightly coat kabobs with vegetable oil. Place on grill for 2 minutes. Turn.

Grill for approximately 2 more minutes until temperature reaches 145°F.

SEASONING

3 garlic cloves, minced
2 T. fresh cilantro, chopped
2 T. olive oil
1 T. lemon juice
2 tsp. ground cumin
1 tsp. paprika
¼ tsp. ground red pepper

Temp: Medium-High   **Heat Source:** Direct

Calculations per Serving:
229 calories
11 gm total fat
1 gm saturated fat
35 mg cholesterol
71 mg sodium

Diabetic Exchanges:
1 vegetable
3 meat

SPECIAL EQUIPMENT
skewers
basting brush
microwave oven
microwave dish

Peppercorn Swordfish Kabobs

1 lb. swordfish, boneless, skinless, cut into 1" chunks
1 small sweet onion, cut into 8 wedges
vegetable oil

SERVES: 4

SUBSTITUTIONS: shrimp, scallops

SEASONING

1¹/₂ tsp. black
peppercorns,
crushed
¹/₂ tsp. paprika
¹/₂ tsp. garlic powder
¹/₄ tsp. salt

Microwave onion in covered microwave dish for 2 minutes.

Mix all seasoning ingredients in Ziploc™ bag.

Add swordfish to seasoning. Seal and shake to coat.

Thread swordfish on skewers, alternating with 2 onion wedges on each kabob.

Using a basting brush, lightly coat kabobs with vegetable oil. Place on grill for 2 minutes. Turn.

Grill for approximately 2 more minutes.

Calculations per Serving:
158 calories
8 gm total fat
1 gm saturated fat
44 mg cholesterol
248 mg sodium

Heat Source: Direct   **Temp:** Medium-High

Diabetic Exchanges:
3 meat

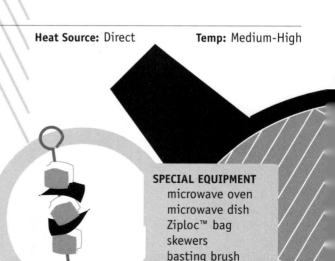

SPECIAL EQUIPMENT
microwave oven
microwave dish
Ziploc™ bag
skewers
basting brush

Rojo Garlic-Lime Shrimp Kabobs

1 lb. large shrimp, peeled, deveined

SERVES: 4   **SUBSTITUTIONS: scallops, tuna, salmon**

Mix all marinade ingredients in Ziploc™ bag.

Add shrimp to bag. Seal and marinate in refrigerator for 15 minutes.

Remove shrimp from marinade. Thread shrimp on skewers.

Place on grill for 2 minutes. Turn.

Grill for approximately 2 more minutes.

MARINADE
- **3 Rojo garlic cloves*, minced**
- **2 T. water**
- **1 T. lime juice**
- **1 T. olive oil**
- **¼ tsp. each salt and pepper**

* Rojo garlic is well worth the hunt. It is much spicier than regular garlic and is full of flavor.

Temp: Medium-High   **Heat Source:** Direct

Calculations per Serving:
129 calories
3 gm total fat
0 gm saturated fat
172 mg cholesterol
204 mg sodium

Diabetic Exchanges:
3 meat

SPECIAL EQUIPMENT
Ziploc™ bag
skewers

Salmon Skewers
with Pesto Sauce

1 lb. salmon, boneless, skinless, cut into 1" chunks
vegetable oil

SERVES: 4

SUBSTITUTIONS: shark, tuna, shrimp

PESTO BASTING SAUCE

2 garlic cloves, minced
¼ C. fresh parsley, minced
¼ C. olive oil
¼ C. lemon juice
1 tsp. dried basil
¼ tsp. salt

Mix all Pesto Basting Sauce ingredients in medium glass bowl.
Arrange salmon on skewers.
Lightly brush salmon with vegetable oil. Place on grill.
Using basting brush, coat salmon with Pesto Basting Sauce during grilling.
Grill for 2 minutes. Turn.
Grill for approximately 2 more minutes.

Calculations per Serving:
163 calories
7 gm total fat
1 gm saturated fat
59 mg cholesterol
113 mg sodium

Diabetic Exchanges:
3 meat

Heat Source: Direct

Temp: Medium-High

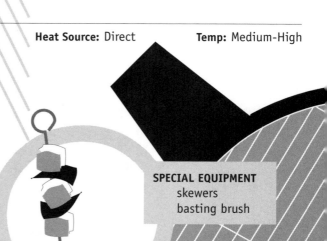

SPECIAL EQUIPMENT
skewers
basting brush

Shark Teriyaki Kabobs

1½ lbs. shark fillets, boneless, skinless, cut into 1" chunks
1 20-oz. can pineapple chunks, drained (reserve 3 T. juice)
1 large green bell pepper, seeded, cubed
vegetable cooking spray

SERVES: 6

SUBSTITUTIONS: swordfish, albacore tuna, marlin

MARINADE

Mix all marinade ingredients in Ziploc™ bag.

Put shark in bag with marinade. Seal and shake to coat. Marinate in refrigerator for 15 minutes.

Remove shark from marinade. Thread on skewers, alternating shark, pineapple, and peppers.

Lightly coat kabobs with vegetable spray. Place on grill for 2 minutes. Turn.

Grill for approximately 2 more minutes.

4 garlic cloves, minced
¼ C. light soy sauce
3 T. reserved pineapple juice
1 T. fresh ginger, grated
1 tsp. honey
½ tsp. dry mustard

Hint: This is spectacular served on a pile of steaming rice!

Temp: Medium-High   Heat Source: Direct

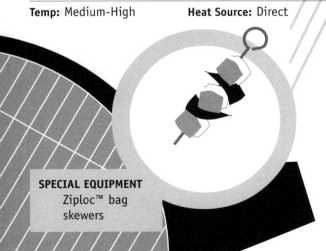

Calculations per Serving:
229 calories
5 gm total fat
1 gm saturated fat
58 mg cholesterol
200 mg sodium

Diabetic Exchanges:
1 vegetable
1 fruit
3 meat

SPECIAL EQUIPMENT
Ziploc™ bag
skewers

Spicy Skewered Scallops
in Peanut Sauce

1 lb. sea scallops
vegetable oil

SERVES: 8

SUBSTITUTIONS: tuna, swordfish

PEANUT SAUCE
¼ C. peanut butter
2 garlic cloves, minced
2 scallions, chopped
3 T. light soy sauce
3 T. rice vinegar
1 tsp. sugar
½ tsp. ground red pepper

Mix all sauce ingredients in medium glass dish.

Add scallops. Cover and marinate in refrigerator for 15 minutes.

Remove scallops from marinade. Thread scallops on skewers.

Using basting brush, lightly coat scallops with vegetable oil and place on grill for 2 minutes. Turn.

Grill for approximately 3 more minutes.

Calculations per Serving:
112 calories
5 gm total fat
1 gm saturated fat
19 mg cholesterol
357 mg sodium

Diabetic Exchanges:
2 meat

Heat Source: Direct

Temp: Medium-High

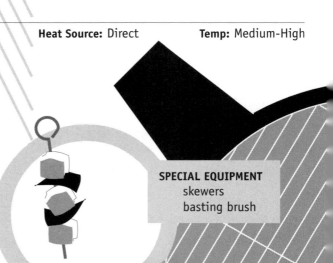

SPECIAL EQUIPMENT
skewers
basting brush

Shrimp on a Stick

4 3-4 oz. each colossal shrimp, shell on*
vegetable cooking spray

SERVES: 4   **SUBSTITUTIONS: slipper lobster tails**

Make two long cuts with a knife through the shell of each shrimp. The cuts in the shell will allow more of the marinade to penetrate the meat.

Mix marinade in bowl. Place shrimp in bowl and marinate in refrigerator for 20 minutes.

Remove shrimp from bowl. Insert metal skewer lengthwise through shrimp. Leave shell and tail on shrimp. Use one skewer for one shrimp.

Coat shrimp with vegetable cooking spray. Grill for 3 minutes per side or just until shrimp turn pink.

Peel shells from shrimp.

You are ready to eat your shrimp off the stick. For a sandwich, remove shrimp from skewer and slice shrimp meat into diagonal pieces.

Cut the hoagie roll in half, leaving one side attached to act as a hinge. Lightly butter bread and lay on grill until toasted.

Spread bread with Thousand Island dressing. Mash avocado in bowl and spread on bread. Lay shrimp meat on avocado and drizzle cocktail sauce over shrimp.

* Leaving the shell on gives the meat more flavor when you grill it. The shell also acts as a natural barrier between the flame and meat.

MARINADE

2 T. lemon juice
2 T. olive oil
2 T. water
2 T. scallions, chopped
$1/4$ tsp. garlic powder
$1/4$ tsp. salt

FIXIN'S

wonderful hoagie rolls
avocado, mashed
Thousand Island dressing
cocktail sauce

Heat Source: Direct

Temp: Medium-High

Calculations per Serving:
146 calories
5 gm total fat
1 gm saturated fat
172 mg cholesterol
205 mg sodium

Diabetic Exchanges:
3 meat

SPECIAL EQUIPMENT
skewers

Chapter 6
Salads

Grilled Salmon Salad

4 salmon steaks
vegetable oil
$1/4$ tsp. each salt and pepper
4 C. mixed greens

1 orange, peeled, seeded,
   chopped
$1/4$ red onion, thinly sliced
2 T. almonds, sliced

SERVES: 4

SUBSTITUTIONS: tuna, triggerfish

DRESSING

4 T. orange juice
2 T. olive oil
dash of cinnamon

Lightly coat salmon steaks with vegetable
   oil. Season with salt and pepper.
Place salmon on grill for 4 minutes. Turn.
Grill for approximately 4 more minutes until
   internal temperature reaches 145°F.
Remove skin and bones from salmon.
Arrange mixed greens on 4 plates. Place
   salmon on greens. Top with orange,
   onion, and almonds.
Mix orange juice, olive oil, and cinnamon in
   small bowl. Pour over salmon and
   greens.

Calculations per Serving:
254 calories
13 gm total fat
2 gm saturated fat
44 mg cholesterol
257 mg sodium

Diabetic Exchanges:
1 vegetable
$1/2$ fruit
3 meat

Heat Source: Direct   **Temp:** Medium-High

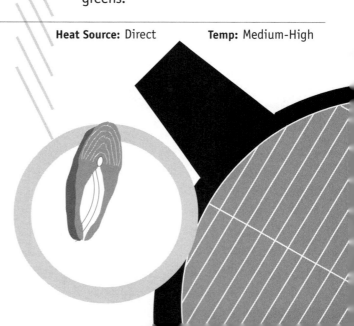

Chinese Tuna Salad

1 lb. tuna, cut into 1" chunks
vegetable oil
¼ tsp. lemon-pepper seasoning
3 C. lettuce, shredded

½ C. carrots, julienne-cut
¼ C. red cabbage, shredded
¼ C. scallions, sliced
½ C. ramen noodles, uncooked, crumbled

SERVES: 6

SUBSTITUTIONS: any leftover cooked fish or shellfish

Lightly coat tuna with vegetable oil. Sprinkle with lemon-pepper seasoning.
Grill tuna on fine wire mesh rack for 4 minutes. Turn.
Grill for approximately 2 to 3 more minutes until internal temperature reaches 145°F.
Whisk all dressing ingredients in large bowl.
Add lettuce, carrots, cabbage, and scallions. Toss.
Add grilled tuna. Toss gently.
Top with crumbled ramen noodles. Serve immediately.

DRESSING
3 T. light soy sauce
2 T. sweet rice vinegar
1 T. olive oil
½ tsp. sesame oil
½ tsp. garlic powder
½ tsp. black pepper

Temp: Medium-High **Heat Source:** Direct

Calculations per Serving:
178 calories
8 gm total fat
1 gm saturated fat
32 mg cholesterol
422 mg sodium

Diabetic Exchanges:
1 vegetable
2½ meat

SPECIAL EQUIPMENT
fine wire mesh rack

Mahi-mahi Salad

**1 lb. mahi-mahi fillets,
cut into 1" chunks**
vegetable oil
$\frac{1}{4}$ tsp. lemon-pepper seasoning

1 head romaine lettuce leaves
$\frac{1}{4}$ C. Parmesan cheese
10 croutons

SERVES: 4

SUBSTITUTIONS: trout, salmon

DRESSING

**$\frac{1}{3}$ C. light Caesar
salad dressing**

Lightly coat mahi-mahi with vegetable oil. Sprinkle with lemon-pepper seasoning.
Grill mahi-mahi on fine wire mesh rack for 1 minute on each side until internal temperature reaches 145°F.
Cut lettuce and put in large bowl.
Toss lettuce with cheese, croutons, and dressing.
Top with grilled mahi-mahi.

Calculations per Serving:
176 calories
4 gm total fat
2 gm saturated fat
48 mg cholesterol
459 mg sodium

Heat Source: Direct

Temp: Medium-High

Diabetic Exchanges:
1 vegetable
3 meat

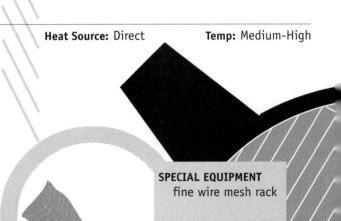

SPECIAL EQUIPMENT
fine wire mesh rack

Salmon Salad
with Lemonade Vinaigrette

1 lb. salmon chunks
vegetable oil
$^1/_4$ tsp. lemon-pepper seasoning

2 C. mixed salad greens
1 orange, peeled, seeded,
  broken into segments
1 grapefruit, peeled, seeded,
  broken into segments

SERVES: 4   SUBSTITUTIONS: tuna, swordfish

Combine all vinaigrette ingredients in
  medium glass bowl. Mix well. Chill.
Lightly coat salmon with vegetable oil.
  Sprinkle with lemon-pepper
  seasoning.
Grill salmon on fine wire mesh rack for 1
  minute on each side until internal
  temperature reaches 145°F.
Arrange greens, orange, and grapefruit on
  4 chilled salad plates.
Top with salmon.
Pour vinaigrette over salmon and fruit.
  Top with Craisins™.

VINAIGRETTE

$^1/_2$ C. lemonade
2 T. olive oil
2 T. Dijon mustard
2 T. chives, chopped
1 serrano chili, finely
  chopped
$^1/_4$ tsp. each salt and
  white pepper

GARNISH

Craisins™

Temp: Medium-High   **Heat Source:** Direct

Calculations per Serving:
274 calories
13 gm total fat
2 gm saturated fat
59 mg cholesterol
383 mg sodium

Diabetic Exchanges:
1 vegetable
$^1/_2$ fruit
3 meat

SPECIAL EQUIPMENT
  fine wire mesh rack

Shrimp and Curry Rice Salad

1 lb. large shrimp, peeled, deveined
vegetable oil
3 C. steamed rice*

1 C. celery, chopped
1 apple, seeded, diced
¼ C. almonds, slivered

SERVES: 4

SUBSTITUTIONS: bay scallops, langostino

DRESSING

1 C. low-fat vanilla yogurt
¼ C. Craisins™
1 tsp. curry powder

Lightly coat shrimp with vegetable oil. Grill on fine wire mesh rack for 3 minutes per side or just until pink.
Mix all dressing ingredients in large bowl. Add rice, celery, apple, almonds, and shrimp to dressing. Stir together.

Preplan leftover rice from the night before.

Calculations per Serving:
412 calories
9 gm total fat
2 gm saturated fat
176 mg cholesterol
239 mg sodium

Heat Source: Direct   **Temp:** Medium-High

Diabetic Exchanges:
1 vegetable
2 bread
1 fruit
3 meat

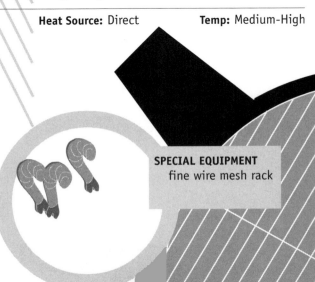

SPECIAL EQUIPMENT
fine wire mesh rack

Shrimp, Tomato, & Mozzarella Salad

1 lb. large shrimp, peeled, deveined
vegetable oil
2 C. zucchini, cubed
1 C. cherry tomatoes, halved
1 C. English cucumber, cubed

$\frac{1}{2}$ C. celery, chopped
$\frac{1}{2}$ C. sweet onion, thinly sliced
$\frac{1}{2}$ C. low-fat mozzarella, cut into strips
2 T. fresh basil, chopped
2 T. fresh parsley, chopped
lettuce leaves

SERVES: 6

SUBSTITUTIONS: shark, swordfish

Lightly coat shrimp with vegetable oil.
Grill on fine wire mesh rack for 3 minutes per side or just until pink.
Combine vegetables, cheese, basil, and parsley in large bowl. Add shrimp.
Mix all dressing ingredients in small bowl.
Drizzle dressing over salad. Gently toss.
Serve on lettuce-lined plates.

DRESSING

3 T. red wine vinegar
1 T. olive oil
1 T. water
$\frac{1}{4}$ tsp. each salt and pepper

Temp: Medium-High   **Heat Source:** Direct

Calculations per Serving:
134 calories
5 gm total fat
1 gm saturated fat
116 mg cholesterol
239 mg sodium

Diabetic Exchanges:
1 vegetable
2$\frac{1}{2}$ meat

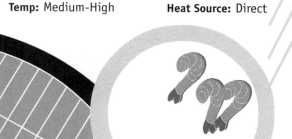

SPECIAL EQUIPMENT
fine wire mesh rack

Spicy Thai Shrimp Salad

1 lb. large shrimp, peeled, deveined
vegetable oil

1 cucumber, peeled, seeded, sliced
1 sweet onion, sliced
salad greens, such as romaine or red leaf lettuce

SERVES: 4

SUBSTITUTIONS: scallops, squid

DRESSING

4 T. lime juice
2 T. sesame oil
2 T. light soy sauce
1 T. sesame seeds, toasted
1 T. fresh cilantro, minced
1 T. fresh mint, minced
$\frac{1}{8}$ tsp. red pepper flakes, crushed

Lightly coat shrimp with vegetable oil.
Grill on fine wire mesh rack for 2 minutes per side or just until pink.
Mix all dressing ingredients in large bowl.
Add shrimp, cucumber, and onion. Toss. Chill.
Place salad greens on 4 salad plates.
Spoon shrimp salad on top.

Heat Source: Direct   **Temp:** Medium-High

Calculations per Serving:
268 calories
11 gm total fat
2 gm saturated fat
172 mg cholesterol
528 mg sodium

Diabetic Exchanges:
1 vegetable
$\frac{1}{2}$ fruit
3 meat

SPECIAL EQUIPMENT
fine wire mesh rack

Summertime Grilled Shrimp Salad

1 lb. large shrimp, peeled, deveined
5 C. fresh spinach, torn
¼ C. walnuts, halved, toasted

8 strawberries, halved
8 asparagus spears, cut into 2" pieces

SERVES: 4   SUBSTITUTIONS: salmon, lobster

Toss shrimp with half of the vinaigrette dressing (¼ C.) in small glass bowl. Cover and marinate in refrigerator for 15 minutes.

Remove shrimp from marinade. Thread on skewers. Grill on fine wire mesh rack for 2 minutes per side or just until pink.

Mix spinach, walnuts, strawberries, and asparagus, and toss with remaining ¼ C. vinaigrette salad dressing. Divide onto 4 salad plates.

Remove shrimp from skewers and lay on salad.

Serve while shrimp are hot.

DRESSING
½ C. vinaigrette salad dressing

Temp: Medium-High   **Heat Source:** Direct

Calculations per Serving:
221 calories
7 gm total fat
1 gm saturated fat
172 mg cholesterol
272 mg sodium

Diabetic Exchanges:
1 vegetable
½ fruit
3½ meat

SPECIAL EQUIPMENT
skewers
fine wire mesh rack

Chapter 7
Fun Food

Alaska Salmon Patties

2 6-oz. cans Alaska salmon, boneless, skinless, drained
vegetable oil

SERVES: 4

SUBSTITUTIONS: canned tuna, surimi, cooked crabmeat

PATTIES

¹/₂ C. Japanese bread crumbs*
¹/₄ C. scallions, sliced
3 egg whites, beaten
2 T. lemon juice
1¹/₂ T. Dijon mustard

Flake salmon in small bowl.
Mix bread crumbs*, scallions, egg whites, lemon juice, and mustard with salmon. Blend well.
Form mixture into 4 patties.
Lightly coat burgers with vegetable oil.
Place burgers on grill lined with heavy-duty aluminum foil for approximately 3 minutes per side until internal temperature reaches 130°F.

Japanese bread crumbs are wonderful, but if you can't find them you can use crushed cornflakes.

Heat Source: Indirect   **Temp:** Medium-High

Calculations per Serving:
202 calories
9 gm total fat
2 gm saturated fat
20 mg cholesterol
254 mg sodium

Diabetic Exchanges:
¹/₂ bread
2 meat

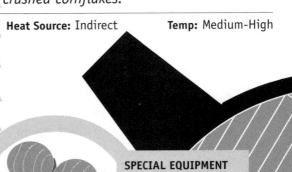

SPECIAL EQUIPMENT
heavy-duty
aluminum foil

Hint: Serve each patty on a bun with lettuce, tomato, and condiments as desired.

Bacon-Mushroom Salmon Burgers

**4 salmon or tuna patties, unthawed
vegetable oil
4 Canadian bacon slices**

SERVES: 4

Lightly coat unthawed patties with vegetable oil.

Place patties on grill for 3 minutes. Turn. Place 1 piece of Canadian bacon on top of each patty.

Grill for approximately 3 more minutes until internal temperature reaches 145°F.

Tear off a sheet of heavy-duty aluminum foil. Fold up sides and ends of foil, about an inch, to make a boat. Combine all Mushroom Sauce ingredients in boat and sauté until mushrooms are tender.

Layer each bun with fish patty, Mushroom Sauce, and lettuce.

MUSHROOM SAUCE

**1 C. mushrooms, sliced
1 T. olive oil
1 tsp. light soy sauce
1 T. brown sugar
2 T. scallions, chopped**

FIXIN'S

**4 toasted burger buns
4 lettuce leaves**

Temp: Medium-High   **Heat Source:** Direct

Calculations per Serving:
418 calories
57 gm total fat
4 gm saturated fat
56 mg cholesterol
717 mg sodium

Diabetic Exchanges:
1 vegetable
2½ bread
2 meat
1 fat

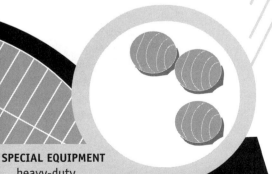

SPECIAL EQUIPMENT
heavy-duty aluminum foil

Clam Pizza

2 6½-oz. cans clams, drained, chopped
1 prepared pizza shell

SERVES: 4

SUBSTITUTIONS: shrimp meat

TOPPINGS

**4 garlic cloves,
  minced**
**½ C. ricotta
  cheese**
1 T. lemon juice
**¼ tsp. garlic
  powder**
**1 C. low-fat
  mozzarella
  cheese,
  shredded**

Place prepared pizza shell directly on grill. Cook for 1 minute or until golden grill marks appear.
Remove pizza shell from grill and turn over. Sprinkle grilled side with minced garlic. Spread clams over top.
Mix ricotta cheese, lemon juice, and garlic powder in small bowl.
Spread over clams.
Sprinkle mozzarella cheese over all.
Place on grill and heat for approximately 4 to 5 minutes or until cheese melts.

Calculations per Serving:
421 calories
11 gm total fat
2 gm saturated fat
67 mg cholesterol
550 mg sodium

Heat Source: Indirect   **Temp:** Medium-High

Diabetic Exchanges:
2½ bread
3 meat

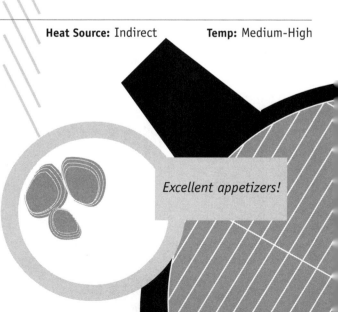

Excellent appetizers!

Crab Quesadillas

1 lb. crabmeat
vegetable oil
1 C. sweet onion, chopped
$1/2$ C. red bell pepper, chopped
$1/2$ C. green bell pepper, chopped

3 T. jalapeño peppers, diced
2 T. fresh cilantro, chopped
$1/4$ C. light cream cheese, softened
2 T. light mayonnaise
$1/4$ tsp. lemon-pepper seasoning

SERVES: 10   **SUBSTITUTIONS: surimi, cooked shrimp**

Lightly coat heavy-duty aluminum foil with vegetable oil. Place foil on grill.

Spread onions and peppers over aluminum foil. Sauté for 10 minutes.

Move foil rack with vegetables to cool side of grill.

Add crab, cilantro, cream cheese, mayonnaise, and lemon-pepper seasoning to vegetables. Carefully stir ingredients together.

Spread crab mixture on half of each tortilla. Sprinkle with cheese and tomato.

Fold tortillas in half and press firmly. Lightly coat with vegetable oil.

Grill tortillas until golden brown and cheese is melted.

Hint: Cut into wedges and serve with salsa for an appealing appetizer. Quesadillas are crowd-pleasers with such broad appeal that they are no longer exclusively on Mexican and Southwest menus. Tortillas are blank canvases that can be filled with innovative ingredients!

WRAP
10 tortillas
$1/2$ C. low-fat Monterey Jack cheese, shredded
1 C. tomatoes, diced

Temp: Medium-High

Heat Source: Indirect/Direct

SPECIAL EQUIPMENT
heavy-duty aluminum foil

Calculations per Serving:
219 calories
7 gm total fat
2 gm saturated fat
38 mg cholesterol
419 mg sodium

Diabetic Exchanges:
1 vegetable
1 bread
2 meat

Maui Seafood Tacos

1 lb. wahoo, boneless, skinless, cut into 8 1"-wide strips
vegetable oil
$\frac{1}{4}$ tsp. lemon-pepper seasoning
$\frac{1}{4}$ C. Japanese bread crumbs*

8 corn tortillas
1 $15\frac{1}{2}$-oz. can fat-free refried beans
2 C. vegetables, such as cabbage, lettuce, or carrots, shredded

SERVES: 8

SUBSTITUTIONS: shark, tuna

MAUI SAUCE

1 C. nonfat plain yogurt, drained
$\frac{1}{4}$ C. fresh cilantro, finely chopped
2 T. jalapeño peppers, seeded, finely chopped
1 tsp. lime juice

Mix all Maui Sauce ingredients in small glass bowl. Refrigerate.
Lightly coat wahoo with vegetable oil. Sprinkle with lemon-pepper seasoning. Roll in bread crumbs.
Grill wahoo on fine wire mesh rack for approximately 1 minute on each side until internal temperature reaches 145°F.
Lightly coat tortillas with vegetable oil and place on grill until grill marks appear.
Remove tortillas from grill.
Lay 1 strip of grilled wahoo on each tortilla. Add beans and vegetables.
Top with Maui Sauce.

Calculations per Serving:
189 calories
2 gm total fat
0 gm saturated fat
21 mg cholesterol
377 mg sodium

Diabetic Exchanges:
1 vegetable
1 bread
2 meat

Heat Source: Direct   Temp: Medium-High

We have friends who head for the restaurant that serves these tacos the minute they get off the plane on Maui. Turn up the Hawaiian music and enjoy them at home!

SPECIAL EQUIPMENT
fine wire mesh rack

*or crushed cornflakes

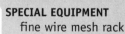

Pizza with Smoked Salmon

3 oz. smoked salmon, sliced or flaked

MAKES 4 six-inch pizzas

Roll pizza dough into 4 circles, each 6"
   across and ¼" thick.
Place the circles of dough directly on the
   grill. Cook for 5 minutes or until
   golden grill marks appear.
Remove from grill.
Spread sour cream on grilled side.
Top with smoked salmon, onions, capers,
   and lemon-pepper seasoning.
Place back on grill until warm.
Cut into appetizer wedges.
Garnish with dill weed.

PIZZA

1 lb. package refrigerated pizza dough
¼ C. light sour cream
¼ C. sweet onion, chopped
2 T. capers, drained
¼ tsp. lemon-pepper seasoning

GARNISH

dill weed

Temp: Medium-High   **Heat Source:** Indirect

Calculations per Serving:
250 calories
11 gm total fat
2 gm saturated fat
10 mg cholesterol
552 mg sodium

Diabetic Exchanges:
2 bread
1 meat
1 fat

Great appetizers!

Seafood Fajitas

1 lb. large shrimp, peeled, deveined

SERVES: 6

SUBSTITUTIONS: squid, firmly textured fish strips

FIXIN'S

6 corn tortillas
vegetable oil
1 sweet onion, sliced
1 red bell pepper, seeded, sliced
1 green or yellow bell pepper, seeded, sliced
¼ tsp. garlic powder
¼ tsp. ground cumin
¼ tsp. lemon-pepper seasoning
desired fillings, such as light sour cream, salsa, lettuce, cilantro, tomatoes, and beans

Wrap tortillas in heavy-duty aluminum foil and place on the grill over indirect heat to warm.

Lightly coat vegetables with vegetable oil and place on fine wire mesh rack over direct heat. Sprinkle with garlic powder, cumin, and lemon-pepper seasoning. Grill for 10 minutes.

Add shrimp to vegetables. Grill for 4 more minutes.

Serve tortillas, shrimp and vegetables, and fillings separately so diners can prepare their own fajitas just to their liking.

Heat Source: Direct/Indirect **Temp:** Medium-High

Calculations per Serving:
155 calories
2 gm total fat
0 gm saturated fat
115 mg cholesterol
167 mg sodium

Diabetic Exchanges:
1 bread
2½ meat

SPECIAL EQUIPMENT
heavy-duty aluminum foil
fine wire mesh rack

Seafood Sausages

4 salmon sausages*
1 sweet onion
vegetable oil

SERVES: 4

Cut onion into 8 wedges, each one held together by a bit of onion root.

Lightly coat onion and salmon sausages with vegetable oil.

Place onion and sausages on grill. Turn frequently.

Grill for approximately 10 minutes until internal temperature of sausages reaches 145°F.

Insert knife through each piece of baguette. Without breaking crust, hollow out enough bread for the sausage to fit in.

Spread mustard through middle of bread.

Put 2 wedges of grilled onion in each baguette. Push the grilled sausage into bread.

FIXIN'S

1 fresh baguette, cut into 4 pieces
Dijon mustard

Salmon sausages may be a little hard to find, but they are well worth the hunt! They are new to the seafood world, so keep your eye out for them!

Temp: Medium-High   **Heat Source:** Direct

Calculations per Serving:
(not available)

Diabetic Exchanges:
(not available)

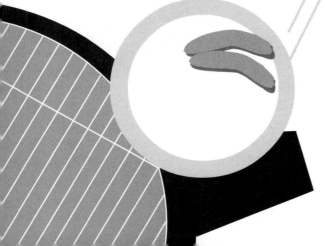

Seared Tuna Sandwiches

4 4-oz. tuna loins
vegetable oil

SERVES: 4

SUBSTITUTIONS: shark, salmon, mahi-mahi

BASTING SAUCE

2 T. orange juice
1 T. olive oil
¼ tsp. lemon-pepper seasoning

FIXIN'S

4 kaiser rolls
4 lettuce leaves
4 tomato slices
4 pineapple slices

Mix all Basting Sauce ingredients in small glass bowl.

Lightly coat tuna with vegetable oil. Place loins on grill and, using basting brush, baste with Basting Sauce. Cook 2 minutes. Turn. Baste again with Basting Sauce.

Cook for 1 to 2 more minutes for medium rare.

Cover rolls with lettuce leaves, and top each with a tomato slice, a pineapple slice, and a grilled tuna loin.

Calculations per Serving:
349 calories
4 gm total fat
1 gm saturated fat
51 mg cholesterol
365 mg sodium

Diabetic Exchanges:
3 bread
3 meat

Heat Source: Direct   **Temp:** Medium-High

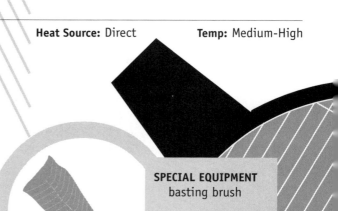

SPECIAL EQUIPMENT
basting brush

Shrimp Wraps

1 lb. medium shrimp, peeled, deveined
olive oil
¼ tsp. lemon-pepper seasoning

SERVES: 8   **SUBSTITUTIONS:** tilefish, mackerel

Lightly coat shrimp with olive oil and sprinkle with lemon-pepper seasoning.

Place shrimp on fine wire mesh rack. Grill for 3 minutes per side or just until pink.

Lightly coat wraps with oil and grill until warm. Remove from heat immediately.

Fill each wrap with shrimp, cabbage, and carrots, and top with a dollop of light ranch salad dressing.

FIXIN'S
8 wraps*
2 C. cabbage, shredded
2 C. carrots, shredded
½ C. light ranch salad dressing

Look for wraps in the tortilla section of the supermarket.

Temp: Medium-High   **Heat Source:** Direct

Calculations per Serving:
220 calories
7 gm total fat
1 gm saturated fat
86 mg cholesterol
404 mg sodium

Diabetic Exchanges:
1 vegetable
1 bread
2 meat

SPECIAL EQUIPMENT
fine wire mesh rack

Swordfish Club Sandwich

1 lb. swordfish, cut into 4 portions
¹/₂ C. light Italian salad dressing

SERVES: 4　　　　**SUBSTITUTIONS: mahi-mahi, halibut**

FIXIN'S

**8 wonderful bread
  slices**
2 T. light mayonnaise
**4 Canadian bacon
  slices**
4 tomato slices
**4 romaine lettuce
  leaves**

Pour Italian salad dressing into Ziploc™ bag.
Add swordfish to dressing. Seal and
  marinate in refrigerator for 15 minutes.
Remove swordfish from marinade. Place fish
  on grill for 3 minutes. Turn.
Grill for approximately 3 more minutes until
  internal temperature reaches 145°F.
Lightly toast bread.
Lay toast on serving plate and spread
  mayonnaise on each slice.
Assemble club sandwiches, starting by
  laying the swordfish on the toasted
  bread. Follow with Canadian bacon,
  tomato, and lettuce.

Calculations per Serving:
331 calories
9 gm total fat
3 gm saturated fat
59 mg cholesterol
848 mg sodium

Diabetic Exchanges:
2 bread
3 meat

Heat Source: Direct　　　　**Temp:** Medium-High

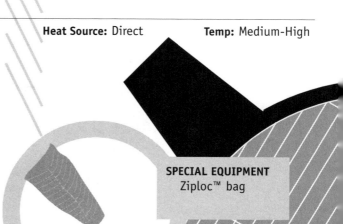

SPECIAL EQUIPMENT
Ziploc™ bag

Teriyaki Salmon Burgers

**4 salmon or tuna patties, unthawed
vegetable oil**

SERVES: 4

Lightly coat unthawed patties with
vegetable oil.
Grill patties for approximately 3 minutes
per side until internal temperature
reaches 145°F.
Mix Teriyaki Sauce ingredients in small
bowl. Spread on toasted buns.
Layer each bun with fish patty,
pineapple, cheese, onion, tomato, and
lettuce.

TERIYAKI SAUCE

**4 T. light mayonnaise
1 T. light soy sauce**

FIXIN'S

**4 toasted burger buns
4 pineapple slices
4 cheese slices
4 onion slices
4 tomato slices
4 lettuce leaves**

Temp: Medium-High   **Heat Source:** Direct

Calculations per Serving:
501 calories
17 gm total fat
4 gm saturated fat
64 mg cholesterol
571 mg sodium

Diabetic Exchanges:
3$\frac{1}{2}$ bread
$\frac{1}{2}$ fruit
3 meat

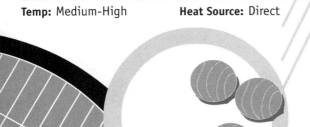

Zesty Salmon Pockets

1 lb. salmon nuggets, boneless, skinless

SERVES: 6

SUBSTITUTIONS: tuna, triggerfish

FIXIN'S

$\frac{1}{2}$ **C. light ranch salad dressing**

$\frac{1}{4}$ **tsp. lemon-pepper seasoning**

vegetable oil

6 pita pockets

2 C. cabbage, shredded

2 C. carrots, shredded

6 tomato wedges

Combine salmon, ranch dressing, and lemon-pepper seasoning in a Ziploc™ bag. Seal and marinate in refrigerator for 15 minutes.

Remove salmon from marinade. Lightly coat with vegetable oil and place on grill for 4 minutes. Turn.

Grill for approximately 3 more minutes until internal temperature reaches 145°F.

Place pita pockets on grill until warm. Remove from grill.

Layer each pita with vegetables on bottom and salmon on top.

Top with a dollop of ranch dressing.

Calculations per Serving:
294 calories
5 gm total fat
1 gm saturated fat
39 mg cholesterol
448 mg sodium

Diabetic Exchanges:
1 vegetable
2 bread
2 meat

Heat Source: Direct   **Temp:** Medium-High

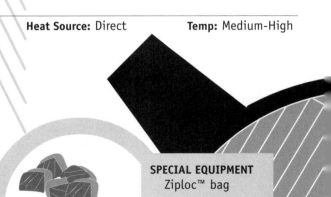

SPECIAL EQUIPMENT
Ziploc™ bag

Lobster Tails For Two

**2 lobster tails (4-6 oz. each) shell-on
vegetable cooking spray**

SERVES: 2   **SUBSTITUTIONS: jumbo shrimp, sea scallops**

Thaw lobster if frozen.
Mix basting sauce in a bowl.
Lobster tails have two sides—the hard,
    cup side and the soft, flat under-
    cover.
Remove soft under-cover of lobster shell.
Insert a metal skewer lengthwise through
    lobster. Use one skewer per lobster.
Coat lobster with vegetable cooking spray
    and place underside down on grill.
Grill for 3 minutes and turn.
Baste with sauce and grill for 3 more
    minutes, or until lobster turns bright
    orange and pulls away from shell.

BASTING SAUCE

$^1/_4$ **C. lemon juice**
$^1/_4$ **C. butter, melted**
$^1/_4$ **tsp. salt**
$^1/_4$ **tsp. pepper**

Temp: Medium-High   **Heat Source:** Direct

Calculations per Serving:
146 calories
5 gm total fat
1 gm saturated fat
172 mg cholesterol
205 mg sodium

Diabetic Exchanges:
3 meat

SPECIAL EQUIPMENT
metal skewers

Chapter 8

Finfish Entrees

After-Work Walleye

4 walleye steaks
vegetable oil

2 C. white wine
$\frac{1}{8}$ tsp. each salt and pepper

SERVES: 4

SUBSTITUTIONS: salmon, pike

GARNISH

Herb Butter (*see Compound Seasoned Butters in Chapter 12*)

Lightly coat walleye steaks with vegetable oil. Place on grill for 4 minutes.

Turn walleye over and place on a sheet of heavy-duty aluminum foil. Fold up sides and ends of foil, about an inch, to make a boat.

Pour wine into foil and bring to a boil. Sprinkle walleye with salt and pepper.

Close grill lid or cover walleye loosely with foil.

Grill for approximately 4 more minutes until internal temperature reaches 145°F.

Garnish top of each walleye steak with slice of Herb Butter.

Calculations per Serving:
123 calories
2 gm total fat
0 gm saturated fat
86 mg cholesterol
53 mg sodium

Heat Source: Direct   **Temp:** Medium-High

Diabetic Exchanges:
$3\frac{1}{2}$ meat

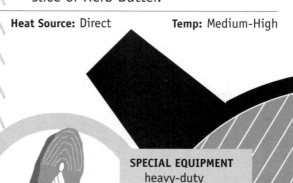

SPECIAL EQUIPMENT
heavy-duty
aluminum foil

Albacore Tuna
with Salsa

4 albacore tuna steaks
vegetable oil

SERVES: 4

¹/₈ **tsp. lemon-pepper**
seasoning

Mix all salsa ingredients in medium glass
bowl. Refrigerate.

Mix all marinade ingredients in flat glass
dish.

Place tuna in marinade. Cover and marinate
in refrigerator for 15 minutes.

Remove tuna from marinade. Lightly coat
with vegetable oil. Sprinkle with lemon-
pepper seasoning.

Place tuna on grill for 4 minutes. Turn.

Grill for approximately 3 more minutes until
internal temperature reaches 145°F.*

Serve with salsa.

*The Western Fishboat Owners Association
recommends an internal temperature of 140°F for
tuna, while many restaurant chefs cook their tuna to
130°F. You can choose which temperatures you'll use
based on the texture and flavor you like best.*

Temp: Medium-High   **Heat Source:** Direct

SALSA

1 C. fresh peaches,
chopped
1 C. fresh plums,
chopped
1 8-oz. can pineapple
chunks, drained
(reserve juice)
¹/₄ **C. red bell pepper,**
finely chopped
2 T. white wine
vinegar
2 T. fresh mint,
minced

MARINADE

reserved pineapple
juice
2 T. olive oil
1 T. light soy sauce
1 fresh lime, juiced

Calculations per Serving:
187 calories
4 gm total fat
1 gm saturated fat
45 mg cholesterol
86 mg sodium

Diabetic Exchanges:
1 fruit
3 meat

SPECIAL EQUIPMENT
heavy-duty
aluminum foil

Basket-Grilled Whole Trout with Bacon

2 whole trout, dressed
vegetable oil

4 bacon strips

SERVES: 4

SUBSTITUTIONS: striped bass, Northern pike, perch

BASTING SAUCE

2 T. Worcestershire sauce
2 T. onion powder
1 T. lemon juice
1 tsp. garlic powder
¼ tsp. salt

Mix all Basting Sauce ingredients in small bowl.

Score skin of trout in three places.

Using basting brush, coat inside and outside of trout with Basting Sauce.

Lightly coat hinged fish basket with vegetable oil.

Lay two strips of bacon in basket. Place trout on top. Top trout with bacon strips and close basket.

Place basket on grill for 4 minutes. Turn. Grill for approximately 4 more minutes until internal temperature reaches 145°F.

Calculations per Serving:
193 calories
10 gm total fat
2 gm saturated fat
69 mg cholesterol
336 mg sodium

Heat Source: Indirect   **Temp:** Medium-High

Diabetic Exchanges:
3 meat

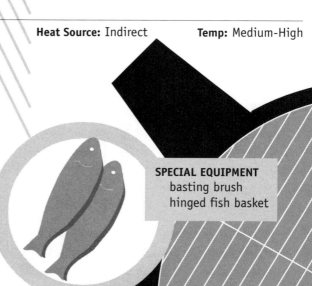

SPECIAL EQUIPMENT
basting brush
hinged fish basket

Bayside Rockfish Packets*

1 lb. rockfish fillet, boneless, skinless, cut into 4 portions

SERVES: 4   **SUBSTITUTIONS: catfish, cod, halibut**

Mix all Vegetable Medley ingredients in large bowl.

Tear off 4 sheets of heavy-duty aluminum foil, each large enough to comfortably wrap around a portion of rockfish.

Divide Vegetable Medley onto sheets of foil. Top with rockfish fillets.

Bring up foil sides. Seal top and ends of foil packets, leaving room inside for good heat circulation.

Grill for approximately 14 to 18 minutes in covered grill.

VEGETABLE MEDLEY

2 red potatoes, sliced
2 T. olive oil
2 T. lemon juice
$\frac{1}{2}$ tsp. garlic powder
$\frac{1}{4}$ tsp. each salt and pepper
$\frac{1}{2}$ C. carrots, chopped
$\frac{1}{2}$ C. celery, chopped

* For fun, you can twist the foil to form a fish-like shape. Twist one end about 3" in from the edge, and flare out the end of the foil to represent the tail. Tuck the other end under to form a point or nose for the fish!

Temp: Medium-High   **Heat Source:** Direct

SPECIAL EQUIPMENT
heavy-duty
aluminum foil

Calculations per Serving:
233 calories
9 gm total fat
1 gm saturated fat
40 mg cholesterol
236 mg sodium

Diabetic Exchanges:
1 bread
3 meat

Hint: *Prepackage and chill—ready to take to the beach and grill on an open-pit barbecue!*

Bluefish Catch of the Bay

1 lb. bluefish fillets, skinless
vegetable oil

SERVES: 4

SUBSTITUTIONS: sablefish, sardines

MARINADE

1 C. light Italian salad dressing

Place bluefish in Ziploc™ bag.
Pour dressing over fillets. Seal and shake to coat. Marinate in refrigerator for 15 minutes.
Remove bluefish from marinade. Lightly coat with vegetable oil.
Place bluefish on grill for 4 minutes. Turn.
Grill for approximately 4 more minutes until internal temperature reaches 145°F.

Calculations per Serving:
155 calories
6 gm total fat
1 gm saturated fat
67 mg cholesterol
213 mg sodium

Diabetic Exchanges:
3 meat

Heat Source: Direct   **Temp:** Medium-High

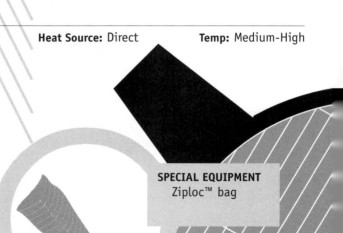

SPECIAL EQUIPMENT
Ziploc™ bag

Cedar-Grilled Whole Salmon

4 to 6 lbs. whole salmon, dressed
¹/₂ tsp. lemon-pepper seasoning

SERVES: 8   **SUBSTITUTIONS: tilapia, bass, catfish**

With knife, make 3 shallow diagonal slashes into both sides of salmon.

Soak cedar plank for at least 30 minutes or overnight. Place salmon on cedar plank.

Sprinkle lemon-pepper seasoning over inside and outside of salmon.

Blend all stuffing ingredients in food processor until finely chopped.

Fill belly cavity with mixture.

Place cedar plank with salmon on grill. Cover.

Grill for approximately 35 minutes until internal temperature reaches 145°F.

Remove skin, bones, and stuffing before serving.

Garnish with lemon wedges and parsley.

Temp: Medium-High   **Heat Source:** Indirect

SPECIAL EQUIPMENT
cedar plank
food processor

STUFFING

1 C. bell pepper (any color), seeded, chopped
1 medium onion, chopped
2 T. olive oil
¹/₂ tsp. garlic powder
¹/₄ tsp. dried thyme
¹/₄ tsp. dried basil
¹/₄ tsp. dried marjoram

GARNISH

1 lemon, cut into wedges
1 C. fresh parsley, chopped

Calculations per Serving:
207 calories
7 gm total fat
1 gm saturated fat
88 mg cholesterol
119 mg sodium

Diabetic Exchanges:
5 meat

Crusted Bluefish
on a Bed of Greens

1½ lbs. bluefish fillets
vegetable oil

¼ tsp. each salt and pepper

SERVES: 6

SUBSTITUTIONS: trout, salmon, mahi-mahi

CRUST

½ C. seasoned
   bread crumbs
¼ C. scallions,
   finely chopped
2 T. Dijon mustard
1 T. olive oil

VEGGIES

3 C. vegetables,
   such as carrots,
   snow peas, or
   mushrooms (all
   with a cooking
   time of about 5
   minutes),
   thinly sliced

Lightly coat bluefish with vegetable oil.
   Season with salt and pepper. Cover
   and refrigerate.
Mix all crust ingredients in medium bowl.
Remove fish from refrigerator. Place on
   grill meat-side down for 4 minutes.
   Turn.
Spread top of fish with crust mixture.
Lightly coat vegetables with vegetable
   oil. Place on a sheet of heavy-duty
   aluminum foil.
Grill fish and vegetables for approximately
   5 more minutes until internal
   temperature of fish reaches 145°F.
Arrange vegetables on serving plate and
   top with fish.

Heat Source: Direct   **Temp:** Medium-High

Calculations per Serving:
229 calories
9 gm total fat
2 gm saturated fat
67 mg cholesterol
468 mg sodium

Diabetic Exchanges:
1 vegetable
½ bread
3 meat

SPECIAL EQUIPMENT
heavy-duty
aluminum foil

Grilled Snapper
and 1015 Onions*

1 lb. red snapper fillets, skinless

1 T. Dijon mustard

1 large, sweet 1015 onion, thinly sliced

1 T. olive oil

SERVES: 4

Toss together all Fruit Relish ingredients. Refrigerate.

Spread both sides of snapper fillets with mustard.

Lightly coat a sheet of heavy-duty aluminum foil with olive oil.

Lay onions on foil and place on grill for approximately 10 minutes until soft and light brown.

Lightly coat snapper with vegetable oil.

Place snapper on grill for 4 minutes. Turn.

Grill for approximately 4 more minutes until internal temperature reaches 145°F.

Place snapper on serving plate. Top with onions and surround with Fruit Relish.

Temp: Medium-High   **Heat Source:** Direct

SPECIAL EQUIPMENT
heavy-duty
aluminum foil

FRUIT RELISH

2 C. orange segments, chopped

1 C. papaya, peeled, chopped

2 T. fresh mint, chopped

¼ C. lime juice

2 T. honey

* 1015 onions are planted on the tenth month and the fifteenth day of that month every fall, hence the name "1015." They are known for their sweetness and for producing minimal bad breath and fewer tears.

Calculations per Serving:
273 calories
5 gm total fat
1 gm saturated fat
42 mg cholesterol
97 mg sodium

Diabetic Exchanges:
2 fruit
3 meat

Grilled Walleye

1 lb. walleye fillets, skin on
vegetable oil

SERVES: 4　　　　**SUBSTITUTIONS: catfish, halibut**

MARINADE

½ **C. red wine**
¼ **C. rice vinegar**
1 T. olive oil
¼ **tsp. garlic**
　powder
¼ **tsp. dried**
　rosemary
¼ **tsp. dried**
　thyme, crushed
¼ **tsp. each salt**
　and pepper

Mix all marinade ingredients in flat glass dish.

Place walleye in dish and marinate in refrigerator for 15 minutes.

Remove walleye from marinade. Lightly coat with vegetable oil.

Place walleye on grill for 4 minutes. Turn. Grill for approximately 3 more minutes until internal temperature reaches 145°F.

Calculations per Serving:
131 calories
3 gm total fat
1 gm saturated fat
98 mg cholesterol
95 mg sodium

Diabetic Exchanges:
3 meat

Heat Source: Direct　　　**Temp:** Medium-High

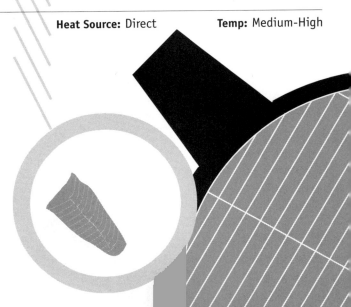

Huka Lodge*
Breakfast Trout

4 trout fillets, skin on
vegetable oil
$1/_8$ tsp. each salt and pepper
2 T. brown sugar

SERVES: 4   **SUBSTITUTIONS:** tilapia, salmon, rockfish

Preheat skillet on grill.

Lightly coat trout with vegetable oil.
   Place on grill meat-side down for 4
   minutes. Turn.

Sprinkle salt, pepper, and brown sugar on
   trout.

Grill for approximately 3 to 4 more
   minutes until internal temperature
   reaches 145°F.

Serve Garlic-Ginger Butter over grilled
   trout.

GARNISH

2 T. Garlic-Ginger
Butter
(see Compound
Seasoned Butters
in Chapter 12)

* Huka Lodge is one of the top-rated small luxury hotels in New Zealand. We had a
delicious trout breakfast there.

Temp: Medium-High   **Heat Source:** Direct

Calculations per Serving:
204 calories
9 gm total fat
1 gm saturated fat
66 mg cholesterol
134 mg sodium

Diabetic Exchanges:
$1/_2$ fruit
3 meat

SPECIAL EQUIPMENT
skillet

Italian Pan-Grilled Lingcod

2 6-oz. lingcod fillets
olive oil

$^1/_4$ tsp. each salt and pepper
$^1/_2$ tsp. garlic powder

SERVES: 2

SUBSTITUTIONS: monkfish, catfish, grouper

ITALIAN SAUCE

1 C. dry white wine
1 14$^1/_2$-oz. can
    Italian-style
    tomatoes,
    drained
1 tsp. dried thyme

Preheat grill pan on grill.
Mix all Italian Sauce ingredients in small glass bowl.
Brush olive oil on lingcod and season both sides with salt, pepper, and garlic powder.
Add lingcod to pan for 4 minutes. Turn.
Pour Italian Sauce into corner of grill pan.
Grill lingcod for approximately 6 more minutes until internal temperature reaches 145°F.
Transfer lingcod to 2 warm plates.
Simmer Italian Sauce for approximately 5 more minutes after removing lingcod.
Pour over fish to serve.

Calculations per Serving:
306 calories
4 gm total fat
1 gm saturated fat
88 mg cholesterol
837 mg sodium

Diabetic Exchanges:
1 vegetable
4$^1/_2$ meat

Heat Source: Direct   **Temp:** Medium-High

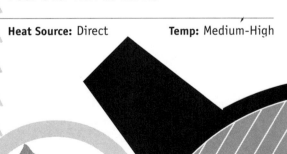

SPECIAL EQUIPMENT
grill pan

Hint: Run hot water over dinner or serving plates for a quick, safe, and easy way to heat them up!

Lemon-Pepper Haddock

1 lb. haddock fillets

SERVES: 4   **SUBSTITUTIONS:** cod, mackerel, salmon

Mix all Basting Sauce ingredients in small glass bowl.

Using basting brush, coat haddock fillets with Basting Sauce.

Place on grill for 4 minutes. Turn. Baste again.

Grill for approximately 4 more minutes until internal temperature reaches 145°F.

BASTING SAUCE

2 T. lemon juice
1 T. olive oil
¼ tsp. lemon-pepper seasoning
¼ tsp. paprika
dash of hot pepper sauce

Temp: Medium-High   **Heat Source:** Direct

Calculations per Serving:
131 calories
4 gm total fat
1 gm saturated fat
65 mg cholesterol
98 mg sodium

Diabetic Exchanges:
3 meat

SPECIAL EQUIPMENT
basting brush

Light and Spicy Shark

1½ lbs. shark fillet, skinless

SERVES: 6

SUBSTITUTIONS: swordfish, marlin, Northern pike

MARINADE

½ C. lemon juice
2 T. olive oil
2 T. prepared horseradish
1 tsp. lemon peel, grated
½ tsp. lemon-pepper seasoning
½ tsp. dried basil
½ tsp. dried oregano

Mix all marinade ingredients in Ziploc™ bag. Reserve 2 T. marinade and set aside.

Place shark in bag with marinade. Seal and shake to coat. Marinate in refrigerator for 20 minutes.

Remove from marinade. Place shark on grill for 4 minutes. Turn. Using basting brush, baste with reserved marinade while grilling.

Grill for approximately 8 more minutes until internal temperature reaches 145°F.

Calculations per Serving:
161 calories
6 gm total fat
1 gm saturated fat
58 mg cholesterol
100 mg sodium

Heat Source: Direct   **Temp:** Medium-High

Diabetic Exchanges:
3 meat

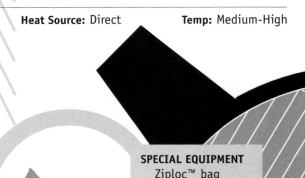

SPECIAL EQUIPMENT
Ziploc™ bag
basting brush

Mediterranean Grilled Swordfish

4 swordfish steaks
3 C. vegetables, such as bell peppers, carrots, eggplant, potatoes, or zucchini (choose vegetables with similar cooking times)
vegetable oil

SERVES: 4   **SUBSTITUTIONS:** sea bass, tuna

Combine all sauce ingredients in saucepan. Simmer for 10 minutes, stirring occasionally.

Lightly coat vegetables with vegetable oil. Place on fine wire mesh rack over grill. Grill for approximately 8 minutes.

Lightly coat swordfish with vegetable oil. Place on grill for 4 minutes. Turn.

Grill swordfish and vegetables for approximately 6 more minutes until internal temperature reaches 145°F.

Arrange swordfish and vegetables on serving plate. Pour sauce over top.

SAUCE

5 garlic cloves, minced
¹/₂ C. vinegar
¹/₂ fresh lemon, juiced
1 T. olive oil
1 T. dried oregano
1 tsp. sugar
¹/₈ tsp. red pepper flakes
¹/₈ tsp. each salt and pepper

Temp: Medium-High   **Heat Source:** Direct

Calculations per Serving:
260 calories
10 gm total fat
2 gm saturated fat
53 mg cholesterol
198 mg sodium

Diabetic Exchanges:
¹/₂ bread
4 meat

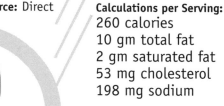

SPECIAL EQUIPMENT
saucepan
fine wire mesh rack

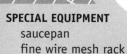

Mesquite-Grilled Salmon Nuggets

1 lb. salmon, boneless, skinless, cut into 1" nuggets
vegetable oil

SERVES: 4

SUBSTITUTIONS: shark, shrimp, tuna

MARINADE

½ C. light soy sauce
⅓ C. honey
1 T. onion powder
1 T. garlic powder
1 tsp. black pepper
3 dashes hot sauce

Mix all marinade ingredients in glass dish.

Add salmon to marinade. Cover and refrigerate for 15 minutes.

Fill chip box with mesquite chips. Place fine wire mesh rack over top of grill rack.

Remove salmon from marinade. Lightly coat with vegetable oil. Lay nuggets over wire mesh rack for 2 minutes. Turn.

Grill for approximately 2 to 3 more minutes until internal temperature reaches 145°F.

Calculations per Serving:
174 calories
5 gm total fat
1 gm saturated fat
59 mg cholesterol
380 mg sodium

Diabetic Exchanges:
½ fruit
3 meat

Heat Source: Direct   **Temp:** Medium-High

SPECIAL EQUIPMENT
chip box
mesquite chips
fine wire mesh rack

Orange Roughy and Mushrooms
in Packets

1 lb. orange roughy, cut into 4 portions

SERVES: 4   **SUBSTITUTIONS:** salmon, flounder, striped sea bass

Tear off 4 sheets of heavy-duty aluminum foil, each large enough to comfortably wrap around a portion of orange roughy.

Center portion of roughy on each sheet of foil.

Spoon mushrooms, scallions, and garlic evenly over each portion.

Fold up sides and ends of foil slightly.

Mix wine, salt, pepper, thyme, and marjoram. Pour evenly over roughy.

Seal top and ends of foil packets, leaving room inside for good heat circulation. Close grill lid or cover packets loosely with foil.

Grill for approximately 9 to 11 minutes.

PACKETS

$1/2$ **lb. mushrooms, quartered**

3 scallions, chopped

2 garlic cloves, minced

3 T. red wine

$1/4$ **tsp. each salt and pepper**

$1/4$ **tsp. dried thyme, crumbled**

$1/4$ **tsp. dried marjoram, crumbled**

Temp: Medium-High   **Heat Source:** Indirect

Calculations per Serving:
170 calories
8 gm total fat
0 gm saturated fat
23 mg cholesterol
221 mg sodium

Diabetic Exchanges:
$2^1/2$ meat

SPECIAL EQUIPMENT
heavy-duty aluminum foil

Pan-Grilled Halibut

1¹/₂ lbs. halibut, cut into 6 portions
vegetable oil

SERVES: 6

SUBSTITUTIONS: cod, grouper, catfish

SHALLOT SALSA

¹/₄ C. shallots,
  minced
1 C. salsa
1 T. olive oil
1 T. lime juice

Preheat grill pan on grill.
Mix all Shallot Salsa ingredients in small glass bowl.
Lightly coat halibut with vegetable oil.
Place halibut in grill pan for 4 minutes. Turn.
Spoon Shallot Salsa over halibut.
Grill halibut for approximately 8 more minutes until internal temperature reaches 145°F.

Calculations per Serving:
159 calories
6 gm total fat
1 gm saturated fat
35 mg cholesterol
372 mg sodium

Diabetic Exchanges:
1 vegetable
3 meat

Heat Source: Direct

Temp: Medium-High

SPECIAL EQUIPMENT
grill pan

Pineapple-and-Ginger-Glazed Swordfish

**1 lb. swordfish loin
vegetable oil**

SERVES: 4   **SUBSTITUTIONS:** salmon, catfish, halibut

Combine all glaze ingredients in
saucepan. Simmer glaze for 10
minutes, stirring occasionally.
Lightly coat fish with vegetable oil. Place
on grill for 4 minutes. Using basting
brush, baste with glaze while grilling.
Turn. Continue to baste with glaze.
Grill for approximately 3 to 4 more
minutes until internal temperature
reaches 145°F.

GLAZE

1 T. olive oil
**1 T. green pepper,
finely chopped**
**1 8-oz. can crushed
pineapple,
undrained**
¼ C. catsup
1 T. light soy sauce
1 T. honey
**1 tsp. fresh ginger,
grated**

Temp: Medium-High   **Heat Source:** Direct

Calculations per Serving:
168 calories
7 gm total fat
2 gm saturated fat
44 mg cholesterol
184 mg sodium

Diabetic Exchanges:
3 meat

SPECIAL EQUIPMENT
saucepan
basting brush

Salmon Plaki Packets

4 salmon fillets, boneless, skinless
4 med. Yukon Gold potatoes, sliced
1 sweet onion, peeled, cut into rings

8 Rojo garlic cloves*, sliced
1/4 C. kalamata olives,
     pitted, chopped
4 T. dried parsley

SERVES: 4   **SUBSTITUTIONS: orange roughy, snapper, halibut**

SAUCE

1 T. olive oil
1/4 tsp. lemon-
     pepper
     seasoning
1 C. low-sodium
     chicken broth
1/4 tsp. dried
     oregano

Tear off 4 sheets of heavy-duty aluminum foil, each large enough to comfortably wrap around a salmon fillet.

Place potato slices flat across foil.

Top potatoes with a salmon fillet.

Lay onion slices over salmon and sprinkle with garlic slices.

Mix olive oil, lemon-pepper seasoning, chicken broth, and oregano. Pour over salmon.

Top with olives and parsley.

Bring up foil sides. Seal top and ends of foil packets, leaving extra room inside for good heat circulation.

Grill for approximately 14 to 18 minutes in covered grill.

Calculations per Serving: **Heat Source:** Direct   **Temp:** Medium-High
451 calories
9 gm total fat
2 gm saturated fat
59 mg cholesterol
204 mg sodium

Diabetic Exchanges:
1 vegetable
3 1/2 bread
3 meat

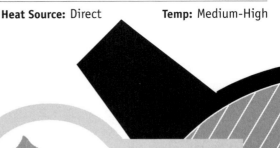

SPECIAL EQUIPMENT
heavy-duty
aluminum foil

* Rojo garlic is well worth the hunt. It is much spicier than regular garlic, and full of flavor!

Salmon Steaks
with Beer Marinade

4 salmon steaks
vegetable cooking spray

SERVES: 4   **SUBSTITUTIONS:** sturgeon, mahi-mahi

Combine all marinade ingredients in Ziploc™ bag. Mix well. Reserve ¼ C. marinade and set aside for basting.

Place salmon in bag with marinade. Seal and shake to coat. Marinate in refrigerator for up to 12 hours. Turn bag occasionally.

Remove salmon from marinade.

Lightly coat salmon with vegetable spray. Place on grill for 4 minutes. Turn. Using basting brush, baste with reserved ¼ C. marinade.

Grill for approximately 8 to 10 more minutes until internal temperature reaches 145°F.

MARINADE
2 C. beer
2 T. brown sugar
1 T. Worcestershire sauce
2 tsp. onion salt
1 tsp. dry mustard

Temp: Medium-High   **Heat Source:** Direct

SPECIAL EQUIPMENT
Ziploc™ bag
basting brush

Calculations per Serving:
151 calories
5 gm total fat
1 gm saturated fat
59 mg cholesterol
206 mg sodium

Diabetic Exchanges:
3 meat

Sashimi*-Seared Tuna Steaks

4 tuna steaks
2 tsp. Cajun Rub *(see Chapter 11)*
vegetable oil

SERVES: 4

Albacore, bluefin, yellowfin, and bigeye are the most common species of tuna sold in the United States. All are firm and mild, with a texture like steak. Your budget may determine whether you sample all the species. Bluefin tuna holds the record for earning a commercial fisherman the most money for one fish: over $25,000.

Lightly coat both sides of tuna with vegetable oil.

Spread Cajun Rub over both sides of tuna.

Place tuna on grill and sear for 3 minutes. Turn.

Sear for approximately 1 more minute until internal temperature reaches 120°F.

Slice thinly and fan tuna out on plate to serve.

Calculations per Serving:
177 calories
7 gm total fat
2 gm saturated fat
43 mg cholesterol
214 mg sodium

Diabetic Exchanges:
3 meat

* *Sashimi is a Japanese dish consisting of small bites of raw fish.*

Heat Source: Direct   **Temp:** High

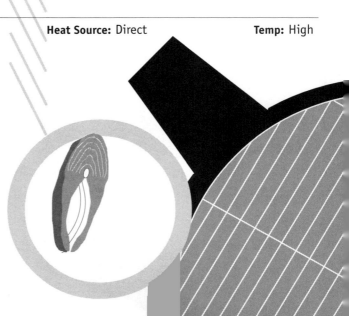

Tuna
with Sautéed Bell Peppers

4 4-oz. tuna loins
4 bell peppers (1 each orange,
   red, yellow, and green),
   seeded, sliced
vegetable oil

$\frac{1}{4}$ C. olive oil
1 tsp. balsamic vinegar
$\frac{1}{4}$ tsp. each salt and pepper
12 black olives, pitted, chopped

SERVES: 4

SUBSTITUTIONS: salmon, swordfish

Lightly coat peppers with vegetable oil.
   Place on fine wire mesh rack over grill
   and sauté for 10 minutes. Remove
   from grill and keep warm.
Brush tuna with 1 tsp. of the olive oil.
   Place on grill for 4 minutes. Turn.
Grill for approximately 4 more minutes
   until internal temperature reaches
   145°F.*
Mix remaining olive oil, vinegar, salt, and
   pepper in bowl. Add olives and
   peppers. Toss.
Top tuna loins with sautéed bell pepper
   mixture.

The Western Fishboat Owners Association recommends an internal temperature of 140°F for tuna, while many restaurant chefs cook their tuna to 130°F. You can choose which of these temperatures you'll use based on the texture and flavor you like best.

Temp: Medium-High   **Heat Source:** Direct

Calculations per Serving:
284 calories
16 gm total fat
2 gm saturated fat
51 mg cholesterol
305 mg sodium

Diabetic Exchanges:
1 vegetable
3 meat

SPECIAL EQUIPMENT
   fine wire mesh rack

Sea Bass
with Spicy Marinade

4 4-oz. sea bass fillets
vegetable oil

SERVES: 4

SUBSTITUTIONS: black cod, bluefish, arctic char

MARINADE

2 garlic cloves, minced
$\frac{1}{4}$ C. light soy sauce
2 T. dry sherry
1 T. honey
1 T. lemon juice
1 T. fresh ginger, minced
2 dashes chili oil

Combine all marinade ingredients in glass dish. Blend well.

Add sea bass to dish and marinate in refrigerator for 15 minutes.

Remove sea bass from marinade. Lightly coat with vegetable oil.

Place sea bass on grill for 4 minutes. Turn.

Grill for approximately 3 more minutes until internal temperature reaches 145°F.

Calculations per Serving:
131 calories
4 gm total fat
1 gm saturated fat
47 mg cholesterol
240 mg sodium

Heat Source: Direct   **Temp:** Medium-High

Diabetic Exchanges:
3 meat

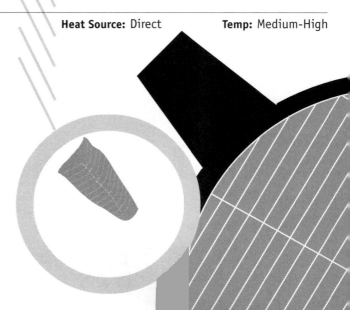

Sea Bass
with Strawberry Salsa

4 sea bass fillets, boneless,
   skinless
olive oil

$1/8$ tsp. garlic powder
$1/8$ tsp. onion powder
$1/8$ tsp. each salt and pepper

SERVES: 4   **SUBSTITUTIONS:** swordfish, mahi-mahi, tuna

Mix all Strawberry Salsa ingredients in
   medium glass bowl. Refrigerate.
Using basting brush, coat sea bass with
   olive oil. Sprinkle seasonings over
   fish.
Place sea bass on grill for 4 minutes.
   Turn.
Grill for approximately 4 more minutes
   until internal temperature reaches
   145°F.
Serve with Strawberry Salsa.

STRAWBERRY SALSA

$1/4$ **C. fresh chopped
   strawberries,**
$1/4$ **C. fresh
   blueberries**
$1/2$ **avocado, chopped**
2 **T. fresh cilantro,
   minced**
1 **T. canned green
   chilies, chopped**
1 **T. orange juice**
2 **tsp. sweet onion,
   minced**
1 **tsp. jalapeño
   pepper, seeded,
   chopped**
$1/4$ **tsp. sugar**
$1/8$ **tsp. salt**

Temp: Medium-High   **Heat Source:** Direct

SPECIAL EQUIPMENT
basting brush

Calculations per Serving:
159 calories
8 gm total fat
1 gm saturated fat
43 mg cholesterol
37 mg sodium

Diabetic Exchanges:
$1/2$ fruit
$2 1/2$ meat

Shark
with Thyme and Shallots

1 lb. shark fillet, skinless
vegetable oil

SERVES: 4

SUBSTITUTIONS: halibut, tuna, mahi-mahi

SAUCE

4 shallots, finely chopped
$\frac{1}{2}$ C. white wine
1 T. water
2 tsp. lemon juice
$\frac{1}{2}$ C. butter
1 T. fresh thyme, chopped
$\frac{1}{4}$ tsp. salt

Heat shallots, wine, water, and lemon juice in saucepan over grill. Stir in butter, thyme, and salt. Simmer sauce over indirect heat while cooking shark.

Lightly coat shark with vegetable oil. Place on grill for 4 minutes. Turn.

Grill for approximately 3 more minutes until internal temperature reaches 145°F.

Pour warm sauce over shark to serve.

Calculations per Serving:
393 calories
31 gm total fat
16 gm saturated fat
123 mg cholesterol
485 mg sodium

Heat Source: Direct/Indirect   **Temp:** Medium-High

Diabetic Exchanges:
3 meat
3 fat

SPECIAL EQUIPMENT
saucepan

Hint: Use olive oil instead of butter to reduce saturated fat!

Arctic Char over Oak

1 lb. arctic char fillet
vegetable oil

SERVES: 4   **SUBSTITUTIONS: trout, salmon**

Mix all marinade ingredients in a shallow glass dish.

Place char meat-side down in marinade. Cover and marinate in refrigerator for 20 minutes.

Fill chip box with oak chips.

Remove char from marinade and lightly coat with vegetable oil. Place char meat-side down on grill for 4 minutes. Turn.

Close grill lid or cover char loosely with heavy-duty aluminum foil.

Roast for approximately 3 to 4 more minutes until internal temperature reaches 145°F.

MARINADE
1 C. white vinegar
$1/4$ C. light soy sauce
$1/4$ C. honey
1 tsp. garlic powder
1 tsp. ground ginger

Temp: Medium-High   **Heat Source:** Direct

Calculations per Serving:
215 calories
10 gm total fat
0 gm saturated fat
0 mg cholesterol
210 mg sodium

Diabetic Exchanges:
$1/2$ fruit
3 meat

SPECIAL EQUIPMENT
chip box
oak chips
heavy-duty
   aluminum foil

Salmon on a Cedar Plank

2 salmon steaks
vegetable oil
$\frac{1}{4}$ tsp. dill weed
$\frac{1}{4}$ tsp. garlic powder
$\frac{1}{4}$ tsp. each salt and pepper

SERVES: 2

SUBSTITUTIONS: striped bass, halibut

Soak cedar plank for at least 30 minutes
(or overnight).
Place plank on grill.
Lightly coat salmon with vegetable oil.
Place salmon directly on grill for 4 minutes.
Turn salmon over and transfer to plank.
Season salmon with dill weed, garlic
powder, salt, and pepper.
Close grill lid or cover salmon loosely with
heavy-duty aluminum foil.
Roast for approximately 10 minutes until
internal temperature reaches 145°F.

Calculations per Serving:
120 calories
5 gm total fat
1 gm saturated fat
44 mg cholesterol
348 mg sodium

Diabetic Exchanges:
3 meat

Heat Source: Indirect   Temp: Medium-High

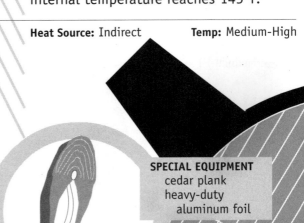

SPECIAL EQUIPMENT
cedar plank
heavy-duty
    aluminum foil

Spicy Rubbed Halibut Steaks

**2 halibut steaks
vegetable oil**

SERVES: 2   **SUBSTITUTIONS:** salmon, tuna, shark

Mix all rub ingredients in small bowl.
Rub both sides of halibut steaks with
   mixture.
Lightly coat halibut with vegetable oil.
   Place on grill for 4 minutes. Turn.
Grill for approximately 8 more minutes
   until internal temperature reaches
   145°F.

RUB

**1 T. olive oil
1 T. lemon juice
$1/_2$ tsp. paprika
$1/_2$ tsp. chili powder
$1/_4$ tsp. dried thyme
$1/_4$ tsp. each salt and
      pepper**

Temp: Medium-High   **Heat Source:** Direct

Calculations per Serving:
166 calories
7 gm total fat
1 gm saturated fat
35 mg cholesterol
209 mg sodium

Diabetic Exchanges:
3 meat

Striped Bass
with Lemon-Rosemary Sauce

4 striped bass fillets
vegetable oil

¹/₈ tsp. each salt and pepper

SERVES: 4

SUBSTITUTIONS: trout, cod, tuna

LEMON-ROSEMARY SAUCE

¹/₄ C. olive oil
4 shallots, chopped
2 T. lemon juice
2 tsp. fresh rosemary, chopped
¹/₂ tsp. sugar

VEGGIES

leafy greens
tomatoes, sliced

Place all Lemon-Rosemary Sauce ingredients in blender. Mix.

Lightly coat fillets with vegetable oil. Season with salt and pepper.

Place meat-side down on grill for 4 minutes. Turn.

Grill for approximately 3 to 4 more minutes until internal temperature reaches 145°F.

Serve immediately on a bed of leafy greens and sliced tomatoes.

Pour Lemon-Rosemary Sauce on top.

Calculations per Serving:
264 calories
20 gm total fat
3 gm saturated fat
91 mg cholesterol
151 mg sodium

Diabetic Exchanges:
3 meat
1 fat

Heat Source: Direct   **Temp:** Medium-High

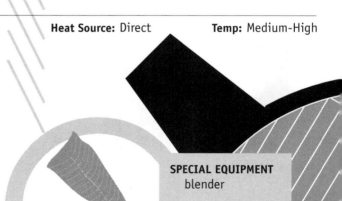

SPECIAL EQUIPMENT
blender

Swordfish
with Roasted Garlic

4 swordfish steaks
2 whole elephant garlic bulbs,
   unpeeled
olive oil

$\frac{1}{4}$ tsp. lemon-pepper
   seasoning
$\frac{1}{4}$ tsp. ground red pepper

SERVES: 4   **SUBSTITUTIONS:** tilefish, sea bass

Put whole garlic on very hot grill.
Lightly coat swordfish with olive oil and
   sprinkle with seasonings. Refrigerate.
After garlic has cooked for approximately
   15 minutes, remove swordfish from
   refrigerator and place on grill for 4
   minutes. Turn.
Grill garlic and swordfish for approximately
   4 to 5 more minutes until internal
   temperature of fish reaches 145°F.
Place cooked swordfish on serving plate.
   Squeeze garlic straight out of cloves
   and spread across top of fish.

Temp: High   **Heat Source:** Direct

Calculations per Serving:
192 calories
7 gm total fat
2 gm saturated fat
53 mg cholesterol
144 mg sodium

Diabetic Exchanges:
$3\frac{1}{2}$ meat

***Hint:** Grilled corn on the cob is a tasty accompaniment.*

Swordfish
with Summer Salsa

4 swordfish steaks
vegetable oil

SERVES: 4

SUBSTITUTIONS: tuna, shark, halibut

SUMMER SALSA

1 C. tomato,
   seeded, chopped
1 avocado, diced
2 T. red onion,
   finely chopped
1 T. jalapeño
   pepper, seeded,
   chopped
1 T. fresh cilantro,
   chopped
1 T. lime juice
1/4 tsp. salt

MARINADE

1/4 C. orange juice
1 T. olive oil
1/8 tsp. onion
   powder
1/8 tsp. garlic
   powder
1/8 tsp. salt

Mix all Summer Salsa ingredients in small
   glass bowl. Cover and refrigerate.
Mix all marinade ingredients in flat glass
   dish.
Place swordfish in dish. Cover and
   marinate in refrigerator for 20
   minutes.
Remove swordfish from marinade.
Lightly coat swordfish with vegetable oil.
   Place on grill for 4 minutes. Turn.
Grill for approximately 4 more minutes
   until internal temperature reaches
   145°F.
Serve with Summer Salsa.

Heat Source: Direct   **Temp:** Medium-High

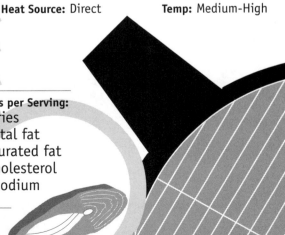

Calculations per Serving:
244 calories
14 gm total fat
3 gm saturated fat
44 mg cholesterol
327 mg sodium

Diabetic Exchanges:
1 vegetable
3 meat

Thai Curried Grilled Salmon
with Spinach

1 lb. salmon, boneless, skinless, cut into 4 portions

2 tsp. curry powder

$^1/_4$ tsp. salt

vegetable oil

SERVES: 4

SUBSTITUTIONS: cod, catfish

Spread curry powder and salt over salmon. Cover and refrigerate.

Heat olive oil in large saucepan. Add spinach, onions, and garlic and sauté for 8 minutes. Transfer to colander and squeeze moisture from spinach.

Place coconut milk, cornstarch, curry powder, salt, and lime juice in same saucepan. Blend. Cook for 6 to 8 minutes on medium heat until thickened, stirring constantly.

Add basil and tomato to saucepan. Add spinach back to pan. Stir. Hold on low heat.

Remove salmon from refrigerator. Lightly coat salmon with vegetable oil.

Place salmon on grill for 4 minutes. Turn.

Grill for approximately 6 more minutes until internal temperature reaches 145°F.

Spoon spinach mixture onto 4 plates and top with grilled salmon.

Temp: Medium-High   **Heat Source:** Direct

SPECIAL EQUIPMENT
large saucepan
colander

SPINACH SAUTÉ

1 T. olive oil

1 bunch fresh spinach

1 C. onion, thinly sliced

4 garlic cloves, minced

1 13$^1/_2$-oz. can light coconut milk

1$^1/_2$ tsp. cornstarch

$^1/_2$ tsp. curry powder

$^1/_4$ tsp. salt

3 T. fresh lime juice

2 T. fresh basil, slivered

1 tomato, seeded, diced

Calculations per Serving:
474 calories
34 gm total fat
21 gm saturated fat
59 mg cholesterol
451 mg sodium

Diabetic Exchanges:
1 fruit
3 meat
2 fat

Tilapia
Grilled in Foil

1 whole tilapia, dressed
¼ tsp. lemon-pepper
  seasoning
2 scallions, cut into strips

2" piece fresh ginger, cut into
  strips
2 garlic cloves, chopped
1 T. light soy sauce

SERVES: 4

SUBSTITUTIONS: trout, salmon

Tear off a sheet of heavy-duty aluminum
  foil, large enough to wrap around the
  tilapia. Center fish in middle of foil.
Sprinkle body cavity with lemon-pepper
  seasoning.
Lay scallions, ginger, and garlic in body
  cavity.
Pour soy sauce over body cavity.
Bring up foil sides. Loosely seal ends and
  top, leaving extra room inside for good
  heat circulation.
Grill for approximately 14 to 18 minutes
  until internal temperature reaches 165°F.

Calculations per Serving:
108 calories
1 gm total fat
0 gm saturated fat
57 mg cholesterol
217 mg sodium

Diabetic Exchanges:
3 meat

Heat Source: Direct   **Temp:** Medium-High

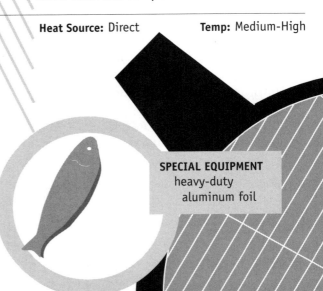

SPECIAL EQUIPMENT
heavy-duty
aluminum foil

Tilapia
with Cucumber Relish

4 tilapia fillets
vegetable oil
$\frac{1}{4}$ tsp. lemon-pepper seasoning

SERVES: 4   SUBSTITUTIONS: trout, salmon, haddock

Combine all relish ingredients in a small
    bowl. Refrigerate.
Lightly coat tilapia with vegetable oil.
    Sprinkle evenly with lemon-pepper
    seasoning.
Place tilapia meat-side down on grill for
    4 minutes. Turn.
Grill for approximately 8 more minutes
    until internal temperature reaches
    145°F.
Spoon relish over tilapia before serving.

RELISH

$\frac{2}{3}$ C. English
    cucumber, seeded,
    chopped
$\frac{1}{2}$ C. radish, grated
2 T. white vinegar
1 tsp. olive oil
$\frac{1}{3}$ tsp. sugar
$\frac{1}{4}$ tsp. dried tarragon
$\frac{1}{8}$ tsp. salt

Temp: Medium-High   **Heat Source:** Direct

Calculations per Serving:
124 calories
3 gm total fat
0 gm saturated fat
57 mg cholesterol
210 mg sodium

Diabetic Exchanges:
3 meat

Trout
with Ginger Basting Sauce

4 trout fillets, skin on
vegetable oil

SERVES: 4

SUBSTITUTIONS: perch, snapper, haddock

BASTING SAUCE

2 tsp. fresh ginger, grated
2 tsp. onion, grated
2 tsp. fresh parsley, chopped
1 tsp. olive oil
1 tsp. light soy sauce

Mix all Basting Sauce ingredients in a small bowl.

Lightly coat trout with vegetable oil. Place meat-side down on grill for 2 minutes. Turn.

Spoon Basting Sauce over fillets while grilling.

Grill for approximately 3 to 4 more minutes until internal temperature reaches 145°F.

Calculations per Serving:
139 calories
6 gm total fat
1 gm saturated fat
57 mg cholesterol
78 mg sodium

Diabetic Exchanges:
3 meat

Heat Source: Direct   **Temp:** Medium-High

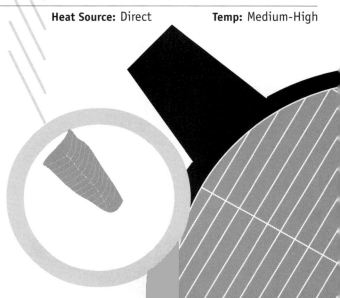

Walnut-Crusted Mahi-mahi

1 lb. mahi-mahi fillets
olive oil

¹/₈ tsp. each salt and pepper
¹/₂ C. chardonnay

SERVES: 4 SUBSTITUTIONS: sea bass, halibut, grouper

Lightly coat mahi-mahi with olive oil. Sprinkle with salt and pepper. Refrigerate.

Mix all crust ingredients in a small bowl.

Remove mahi-mahi from refrigerator and place meat-side down on grill for 4 minutes.

Turn mahi-mahi over and place on a sheet of heavy-duty aluminum foil, skin-side down. Fold up sides and ends of foil, about an inch, to make a boat. Pour chardonnay over mahi-mahi.

Sprinkle top of mahi-mahi with walnut crust. Close grill lid or cover mahi-mahi loosely with foil.

Grill for approximately 4 more minutes until internal temperature reaches 145°F.

CRUST

1 C. walnuts, finely chopped
1 T. fresh basil, chopped
1 T. fresh chives, chopped
1 T. olive oil
1 T. lemon juice

Temp: Medium-High **Heat Source:** Direct

Calculations per Serving:
346 calories
23 gm total fat
2 gm saturated fat
42 mg cholesterol
154 mg sodium

Diabetic Exchanges:
3¹/₂ meat
2 fat

SPECIAL EQUIPMENT
heavy-duty
aluminum foil

Chapter 9
Shellfish Entrees

Barbecued Oysters
in the Shell

12 large, 20 medium, or 32 small oysters in the shell

SERVES: 4

SAUCE

Snappy Barbecue Sauce or Honey Barbecue Basting Sauce *(see Chapter 11)*

* Oysters in the shell have two sides: a lid that is flat and a cup that is bowl-shaped. To make sure the natural juices in the oysters are retained, be sure to place them on the grill with the lid side up.

Scrub oyster shells thoroughly with a scrub brush.

Crumple a sheet of heavy-duty aluminum foil, place on grill, and lay oysters lid side up* in indentations of foil. (Indentations will keep oysters from tipping and spilling their liquid.)

Grill for 5 to 15 minutes or until shells begin to open. (The larger the oyster, the longer the cooking time.)

Place an oyster knife under the lid of each oyster and pry off the top shell.

Top with Snappy Barbecue Sauce or Honey Barbecue Basting Sauce.

Calculations per Serving:
90 calories
3 gm total fat
0 gm saturated fat
45 mg cholesterol
90 mg sodium

Diabetic Exchanges:
1 meat

Heat Source: Direct   **Temp:** Medium-High

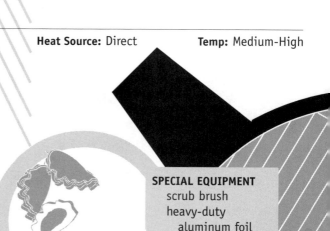

SPECIAL EQUIPMENT
scrub brush
heavy-duty
   aluminum foil
oyster knife

Clams with Vegetable Pesto

24 littleneck, Manila, or Venus clams in the shell
or
12 cherrystone clams in the shell

SERVES: 4   **SUBSTITUTIONS:** mussels in shell

Blend all Vegetable Pesto ingredients in small bowl. Set aside.

Scrub clams in cold water with a scrub brush.

Arrange clams in grill-and-shake basket. Place on grill until shells pop open.

Serve hot grilled clams with a dish of Vegetable Pesto.

VEGETABLE PESTO
1 carrot, minced
1 celery stalk, minced
2 T. scallion, minced
2 garlic cloves, minced
$\frac{1}{4}$ C. olive oil
2 T. lemon juice
$\frac{1}{4}$ tsp. each salt and pepper

Temp: Medium-High   **Heat Source:** Direct

Calculations per Serving:
196 calories
14 gm total fat
2 gm saturated fat
29 mg cholesterol
208 mg sodium

Diabetic Exchanges:
1 vegetable
$1\frac{1}{2}$ meat
1 fat

SPECIAL EQUIPMENT
scrub brush
grill-and-shake basket

Ginger Shrimp
with Asparagus

1 lb. shrimp, peeled, deveined
vegetable oil
1 lb. fresh asparagus

SERVES: 4

GINGER SAUCE

2 T. light soy sauce
2 garlic cloves,
   minced
1 T. sweet rice
   vinegar
1 T. fresh ginger,
   grated
$1/4$ tsp. red pepper
   flakes, crushed
$1/4$ tsp. sesame oil

Butterfly-cut shrimp. Refrigerate.
Clean and trim asparagus. Refrigerate.
Mix all Ginger Sauce ingredients in small
   glass bowl. Set aside at room
   temperature.
Lightly coat asparagus with vegetable oil.
   Place on fine wire mesh rack for 7
   minutes, rotating spears.
Lightly coat shrimp with vegetable oil.
   Grill on wire rack for 2 minutes per
   side or just until pink.
Transfer asparagus and shrimp to serving
   platter.
Pour Ginger Sauce over vegetables and
   shrimp.

Calculations per Serving:
179 calories
5 gm total fat
1 gm saturated fat
172 mg cholesterol
486 mg sodium

Diabetic Exchanges:
1 vegetable
$3^1/_2$ meat

Heat Source: Direct   **Temp:** Medium-High

SPECIAL EQUIPMENT
fine wire mesh rack

*Hint: You can steam green beans
for 4 to 5 minutes as an alternative
to asparagus.*

Italian Grilled Shrimp and Pasta

1 lb. large shrimp, peeled, deveined
olive oil
1/4 tsp. salt
3/4 lb. uncooked pasta

SERVES: 4   **SUBSTITUTIONS:** scallops

Cook pasta in saucepan according to package directions. Drain. Keep warm.

Lightly coat shrimp with olive oil and season with salt. Grill on fine wire mesh rack for 2 minutes per side or until shrimp just turn pink.

Mix spaghetti sauce and oregano in small saucepan. Bring to bubbling boil.

Reduce heat and simmer.

Place pasta in serving bowl. Gently mix in spaghetti sauce. Add shrimp. Toss.

PASTA SAUCE

2 C. Italian-style spaghetti sauce
1 T. dried oregano

Temp: Medium-High   **Heat Source:** Direct

SPECIAL EQUIPMENT
saucepan
fine wire mesh rack

Calculations per Serving:
526 calories
7 gm total fat
1 gm saturated fat
174 mg cholesterol
915 mg sodium

Diabetic Exchanges:
4 bread
1 fruit
3 meat

Mediterranean Squid

1 lb. squid steaks, cut into ¼"-wide strips
vegetable oil

SERVES: 4

MEDITERRANEAN SAUCE

1 T. olive oil
½ C. sweet onion, chopped
2 garlic cloves, minced
2 16-oz. cans Italian-style tomatoes, drained, chopped
½ C. black olives, pitted, sliced
½ tsp. dried oregano
¼ tsp. dried marjoram
⅛ tsp. red pepper flakes, crushed

GARNISH

parsley

Calculations per Serving:
245 calories
8 gm total fat
1 gm saturated fat
264 mg cholesterol
605 mg sodium

Diabetic Exchanges:
1 fruit
3 meat

Hint: Serve with lots of fresh, crusty bread!

Heat olive oil in saucepan. Add onions and garlic. Sauté until lightly brown.
Add tomatoes, olives, oregano, marjoram, and red pepper. Bring to a boil.
Reduce heat, cover, and let simmer.
Lightly coat squid strips with vegetable oil. Grill on fine wire mesh rack for 1 minute.
Pour Mediterranean Sauce into 4 individual bowls.
Top with grilled squid.
Garnish with parsley.

Heat Source: Direct   **Temp:** Medium-High

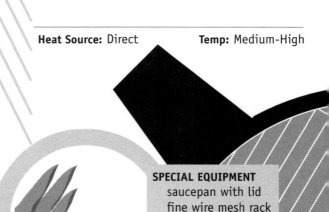

SPECIAL EQUIPMENT
saucepan with lid
fine wire mesh rack

Mussels
in Chive-Parsley Spread

24 to 36 mussels in the shell

SERVES: 4

SUBSTITUTIONS: clams and oysters in the shell

Scrub and debeard mussels with a scrub brush.

Mix all Chive-Parsley Spread ingredients in small bowl. Cover and refrigerate.

Spread a thick layer of rock salt on the bottom of a cast-iron grill pan. Press mussels into salt.

Place pan on grill. Heat pan to medium-high.

Drop a spoonful of Chive-Parsley Spread into each mussel as it opens its shell.

Grill until spread is melted.

CHIVE-PARSLEY SPREAD

$^1/_2$ **C. butter, softened**

$^1/_2$ **C fresh parsley, minced**

$^1/_4$ **C. fresh chives, minced**

Temp: Medium-High   **Heat Source:** Direct

Calculations per Serving:
162 calories
9 gm total fat
4 gm saturated
80 mg cholesterol
387 mg sodium

Diabetic Exchanges:
(not available)

SPECIAL EQUIPMENT
scrub brush
rock salt*
cast-iron grill pan

Crumpled aluminum foil on a small mesh grid works, too.

Shrimp
on a Bed of Sautéed Vegetables

1 lb. large shrimp, peeled, deveined
1 T. olive oil
2 C. red bell pepper, seeded, chopped
2 C. sweet onion, chopped
1 tsp. jalapeño pepper, seeded, minced
6 garlic cloves, minced

⅓ C. lime juice
1 10-oz. pkg. frozen corn
1 16-oz. can black beans, drained, rinsed
1 tsp. cumin
¼ tsp. pepper
vegetable oil

SERVES: 4

SUBSTITUTIONS: scallops

GARNISH

2 T. fresh cilantro, chopped

Hint: To speed preparation at dinnertime, sauté vegetables ahead of time and reheat in the microwave.

Heat oil in grill pan. Add peppers, onions, jalapeños, garlic, and lime juice. Sauté for 3 minutes.

Add corn and black beans. Gently stir in cumin and pepper. Cover pan and remove from heat.

Lightly coat shrimp with vegetable oil and grill on fine wire mesh rack for 2 minutes per side or just until pink.

Divide vegetable medley onto 4 plates to make a bed of vegetables. Top with shrimp. Garnish with cilantro.

Calculations per Serving:
338 calories
8 gm total fat
1 gm saturated fat
172 mg cholesterol
431 mg sodium

Heat Source: Direct   **Temp:** Medium-High

Diabetic Exchanges:
1 vegetable
2½ bread
4½ meat

SPECIAL EQUIPMENT
grill pan
fine wire mesh rack

Snow Crab
with Basting Sauce

1½ lbs. snow crab legs

SERVES: 4

Rinse crab legs under cool water. Cut into 4 portions. Split back of legs. Open each split so it is wide enough to spoon in Basting Sauce.

Mix all Basting Sauce ingredients in small bowl.

Place crab legs split side up on grill. Using basting brush, baste with sauce while grilling.

Grill 3 to 4 minutes until legs are heated.

BASTING SAUCE

2 T. lemon juice
2 T. dry white wine
1 T. olive oil
1 T. fresh parsley, finely minced
1 tsp. lemon peel, finely grated
¼ tsp. white pepper

Hint: If a snow crab has a red shell, it is already cooked—you are only warming it up on the grill.

Temp: Medium   **Heat Source:** Direct

Calculations per Serving:
83 calories
2 gm total fat
0 gm saturated fat
50 mg cholesterol
251 mg sodium

Diabetic Exchanges:
1½ meat

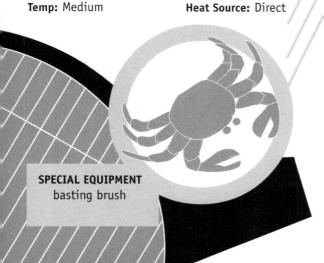

SPECIAL EQUIPMENT
basting brush

Soft-Shelled Crab
on a Bed of Spinach

4 soft-shelled crabs, cleaned
vegetable oil
$^1/_4$ tsp. each salt and pepper
4 C. spinach leaves, washed, dried

1 C. carrots, grated
1 C. grapes, halved
$^1/_3$ C. light poppy seed
   dressing

SERVES: 4

Lightly coat crabs with vegetable oil.
   Season with salt and pepper.
Place crabs upside down on grill for 4
   minutes. Turn.
Grill for 4 more minutes.
Divide spinach, carrots, and grapes on 4
   plates. Place crab on top.
Drizzle poppy seed dressing over top.

Heat Source: Direct   **Temp:** Medium-High

Calculations per Serving:
128 calories
3 gm total fat
0 gm saturated fat
50 mg cholesterol
461 mg sodium

Diabetic Exchanges:
$^1/_2$ fruit
$2^1/_2$ meat

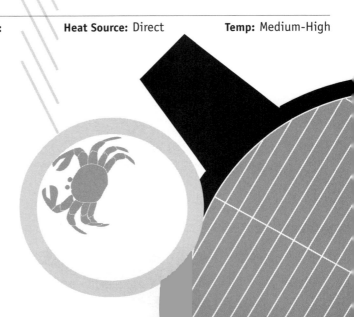

Thai Cilantro Shrimp

1 lb. large shrimp, peeled, deveined

SERVES: 4

Combine all marinade ingredients in blender. Whirl on high until pureed.

Pour marinade into Ziploc™ bag. Place shrimp in bag and marinate in refrigerator for 20 minutes.

Remove shrimp from marinade. Grill on fine wire mesh rack for 2 minutes per side or until shrimp just turn pink.

MARINADE

1 C. cilantro, chopped
$^1/_4$ C. low-fat buttermilk
$^1/_4$ C. flaked coconut
2 garlic cloves, chopped
$^1/_4$ tsp. each salt and pepper

Temp: Medium-High   **Heat Source:** Direct

Calculations per Serving:
131 calories
2 gm total fat
1 gm saturated fat
172 mg cholesterol
210 mg sodium

Diabetic Exchanges:
3 meat

SPECIAL EQUIPMENT
Ziploc™ bag
fine wire mesh rack

Chapter 10
Fishermen's Favorites

Alder Plank–Grilled Wild Salmon

2 wild king salmon steaks

SERVES: 2

1 T. olive oil
¹/₂ tsp. each salt and pepper
1 fresh lemon, juiced

Soak alder plank in water for at least 30 minutes (or overnight).
Lightly coat salmon with olive oil.
Sprinkle both sides of salmon with salt and pepper.
Place plank on grill over indirect heat.
Place salmon directly on grill over direct heat for 4 minutes to sear. Transfer salmon to plank, turning grilled-side up.
Sprinkle lemon juice over salmon.
Grill for approximately 20 more minutes until internal temperature reaches 145°F.

Doug Hatfield,
F/V *Leonard*

Doug started fishing with his father off the Pacific coast of Washington at the age of 10. He has been the skipper on several fishing vessels harvesting Dungeness crab, every species of wild salmon, black cod, herring, and numerous species of rockfish. Doug makes his own wood grilling planks, which are approximately 1" thick.

Heat Source: Indirect   **Temp:** Medium-High

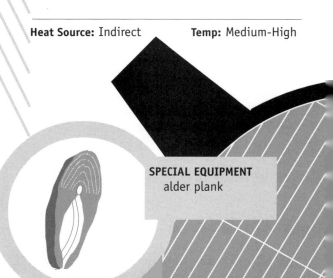

SPECIAL EQUIPMENT
alder plank

Grilled Maine Lobster Tails

4 live Maine lobsters

SERVES: 4

Quickly immerse lobsters head first into a large pot of boiling water for 1 minute.

Remove from water. Snap off tails.

Using culinary shears, remove and discard the undershell of the tail section.

Insert a skewer lengthwise through the hard shell at both ends to prevent curling. (As an alternative, you may clamp the lobster tails tightly in a hinged fish basket.)

Place lobsters shell-side down on grill for 4 to 5 minutes. Turn.

Grill for approximately 5 to 6 minutes until meat is opaque.

Turn lobster shell-side down to serve, and baste meat with a Compound Seasoned Butter and lemon juice.

GARNISH

Compound Seasoned Butter (see Chapter 12)

lemon wedges

Temp: Medium   **Heat Source:** Direct

Gregory Griffin, Lobsterman

SPECIAL EQUIPMENT
large pot
culinary shears
skewers or
   hinged fish basket

Hint: The Maine Lobster Council generally recommends a 165°F internal temperature for whole lobster.

Barbecued Alaska Halibut Pizza

1 lb. halibut, grilled, flaked

SERVES: 6

---

1 T. olive oil
2 sweet onions, peeled, chopped
5 garlic cloves, minced
¹/₃ C. salsa
²/₃ C. Bulls Eye Original™ BBQ Sauce
³/₄ C. walnuts, toasted
1¹/₂ C. cheese (mozzarella, cheddar, and feta), grated (you choose the proportions)
1 16" pizza crust

Hint: *"Grill once, eat twice." Preplan leftovers. Grill twice as much halibut as you need for dinner and save half for pizza.*

Place a sheet of heavy-duty aluminum foil over direct heat on grill. Pour olive oil on foil.

Grill onions on foil for approximately 15 to 20 minutes until caramelized.

Grill one side of pizza crust over indirect heat for approximately 2 minutes. Transfer the crust to a cookie sheet, with the grill marks up.

Spread garlic, salsa, and barbecue sauce on crust.

Layer onions and grilled halibut over sauce. Sprinkle walnuts and cheese over pizza.

Transfer pizza to grill over indirect heat. Close grill lid or cover pizza loosely with aluminum foil.

Grill for approximately 3 to 4 minutes or until cheese is melted.

Wendy Alderson,
F/V Kati J
Sitka, Alaska

Heat Source: Direct/Indirect   **Temp:** Medium-High
Special Equipment: heavy-duty aluminum foil
cookie sheet

Wendy's Barbecued Alaska Halibut Pizza has made her famous during her years of working on commercial fishing boats out of Sitka, Alaska. "When I'm not in a hurry, I make this pizza on the grill with a homemade crust. When the fish are biting, I throw the pizza in the oven." These days Wendy and her husband fish on their troller, a longliner called the F/V Kati J out of Alaska. They sell their frozen-at-sea salmon, halibut, and black cod through Seafood Producers Cooperative (SPC), the oldest seafood cooperative in the United States that deals only with wild fish. Chefs all across the country demand SPC products because of their unsurpassed quality.

Canadian Bacon– Wrapped Barbecued Albacore

1 lb. albacore tuna, cut into 12 chunks
¹/₃ C. light Italian salad dressing
¹/₃ C. teriyaki sauce
12 Canadian bacon slices

SERVES: 4

Mix salad dressing, teriyaki sauce, and albacore in a glass bowl. Marinate in refrigerator for 20 minutes.

Remove albacore from marinade. Wrap a slice of bacon around each chunk of albacore and secure each with 2 heavy-duty toothpicks.

Place on grill for 2 minutes. Turn.

Grill for 3 more minutes or until fish turns opaque (albacore is more moist and tender when cooked to retain a pink-pearl center) and internal temperature reaches 125°F.

Temp: Medium-High   **Heat Source:** Direct

SPECIAL EQUIPMENT
24 heavy-duty toothpicks

Doug Dirkse,
F/V Olinka

Doug once appeared on a PBS television program with the fish he caught on his trolling boat in California. Albacore has a mild taste and will take a variety of spices.

Greek-Style Grilled Sardines

2 lbs. (2) Pacific sardines, whole, headed, gutted

SERVES: 2　　　　　**SUBSTITUTIONS: trout**

MARINADE

1/2 C. olive oil
2 lemons, juiced
5 garlic cloves, minced
1/4 C. fresh parsley, chopped
1/2 C. fresh oregano, chopped

Mix all marinade ingredients in shallow glass bowl. Add sardines to bowl and, if necessary, add water to cover them.
Marinate sardines in refrigerator for at least 30 minutes.
Remove sardines from marinade.
Place sardines in hinged fish basket. Place on grill for 4 minutes. Turn.
Grill for approximately 5 more minutes until internal temperature reaches 145°F.
Serve with Vegetable Medley *(facing page)*.

Heat Source: Direct　　　　**Temp:** Medium-High

SPECIAL EQUIPMENT
hinged fish basket

Vegetable Medley

¼ red onion, chopped
1 red bell pepper, chopped
1 C. spinach leaves, chiffonaded
(cut into strips)
2 tomatoes, seeded, cut into chunks

12 kalamata olives,
pitted, chopped
3 T. olive oil
3 garlic cloves, minced
1 T. fresh oregano, minced

SERVES: 2

Mix onion, pepper, spinach, tomato, and olives in a bowl.

Heat olive oil, garlic, and fresh oregano in saucepan until warm. Pour over vegetables in bowl. Stir gently.

Put half of warm vegetables on each plate. Lay grilled sardines *(facing page)* on top.

Garnish top of sardines with remaining vegetables.

Sardines are back!
The Pacific Ocean from California to British Columbia, Canada, has the potential for harvesting sardines in quantities as large as in the 1930s. The sardines disappeared and fishermen were blamed, but recent research suggests that changes in ocean temperature may have had as much or more to do with the disappearance as did overfishing. Fisheries biologists are closely monitoring today's harvest. In the meantime, Americans have forgotten the delicious taste of grilled sardines, although they remain an important part of the Mediterranean diet.

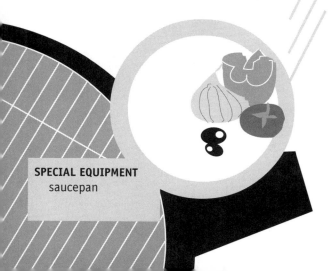

SPECIAL EQUIPMENT
saucepan

Helen's Barbecue Sauce

½ C. catsup
½ C. coffee
¼ C. sugar
¼ C. Worcestershire sauce
1 T. vinegar
1 T. onion, grated

Mix all ingredients in saucepan. Simmer for 15 minutes.
Use as a basting or dipping sauce.

Helen Wagner,
F/V Helen

Helen is a wonderful cook, a great deckhand, and a dedicated fisherman's wife. I met her when we were both fishing for wild salmon off the Pacific coast. I have used her recipe over and over. Yes, coffee is an important ingredient! Starbucks wasn't around when I first tasted this, and Helen confesses that she uses . . . instant coffee.

SPECIAL EQUIPMENT
saucepan

Kasu Salmon*

1 lb. salmon, cut into 4 portions

SERVES: 4   **SUBSTITUTIONS:** sablefish

Mix all kasu ingredients together in large, flat glass dish.
Add salmon to kasu.
Cover and marinate in refrigerator for at least 1 hour (or overnight).
Remove salmon from marinade.
Place salmon on grill for 3 minutes. Turn.
Grill approximately 4 to 5 more minutes until internal temperature reaches 145°F.

KASU

6 T. red miso
3 T. white wine
3 T. soy sauce
1½ T. honey
1 T. sesame oil
1 tsp. fresh ginger, grated
2 garlic cloves, minced

* Kasu is a Japanese term for marinating fish in preparation for grilling or broiling. Miso, a product made from soy, develops a delightful aroma and flavor that transforms simple grilling into a gourmet delight.

Temp: Medium-High   **Heat Source:** Direct

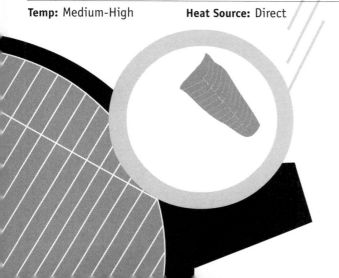

Chapter 11

Marinades, Rubs, & Sauces

Marinating Tips

- A marinade can be a griller's best friend. A marinade adds a variety of taste sensations—spicy, sweet, sour, smoky—to cooking, and can double as a basting sauce. Any liquid used in the marinade will protect your seafood from drying out during grilling. Ask yourself what flavor base you like on chicken, and I'll bet you will love it on seafood, too!
- Marinades may be cooked or uncooked before using. Cooked marinades must be completely cooled before adding to seafood.
- Always marinate in the refrigerator.
- Always marinate in a nonmetal container when using an acid (lemon or lime juice, vinegar, and the like). The acid causes a chemical reaction with metal, which will give your seafood a metallic taste and will discolor the pan.
- Ziploc™ bags are a perfect throwaway container for marinating.
- Most seafood needs to marinate for only 15 minutes. The longer you marinate, the stronger the flavor. Seafood has very little connective tissue and is naturally tender, so a marinade is used just to impart flavor.
- For fillets, choose a container that is just big enough to lay the seafood flat. If you plan to turn the fish while marinating, the marinade needs to cover only one-half of the thickness of the seafood. If you are not going to turn the fish over while marinating, be sure to have enough marinade to cover the seafood. One cup of marinade is generally ample for 1 to $1\frac{1}{2}$ pounds of seafood.
- Marinades with high sugar content will burn easily while grilling, so brush on only during the last few minutes of grilling, or grill indirectly.
- Marinades that come in contact with raw seafood must be thrown away after marinating.
- Set aside 2 or 3 tablespoons of marinade before it comes in contact with raw seafood to serve as a sauce.
- Remove frozen seafood from the freezer, add marinade, refrigerate, and the seafood will thaw and marinate at the same time.
- Make marinade ahead of time (3 days), refrigerate, and on grilling day, you're ready!
- Double the marinade recipe and freeze half in a Ziploc™ bag. To use, pull the marinade out of the freezer, thaw, and use as directed.

Balsamic-Shallot Marinade

½ **C. balsamic vinegar**
2 **T. olive oil**
2 **T. shallots, minced**
1 **tsp. dried sage**
1 **tsp. dried rosemary**
¼ **tsp. lemon-pepper**
    seasoning

Mix all ingredients in medium
    plastic container. Cover and
    refrigerate.

Makes Marinade for 1 lb. of Seafood

CALCULATIONS BASED ON 4 SERVINGS
24 calories   2 gm total fat
0 gm saturated fat   0 mg cholesterol
120 mg sodium

Basil-Parmesan Marinade

2 **scallions, chopped**
1 **C. fresh basil, minced**
¼ **C. lime juice**
2 **T. olive oil**
2 **T. Parmesan cheese, grated**

Combine all ingredients in
    blender. Process until finely
    chopped. Cover and
    refrigerate.

Makes Marinade for 1 lb. of Seafood

CALCULATIONS BASED ON 4 SERVINGS
20 calories   2 gm total fat
0 gm saturated fat   0 mg cholesterol
12 mg sodium

SPECIAL EQUIPMENT: blender

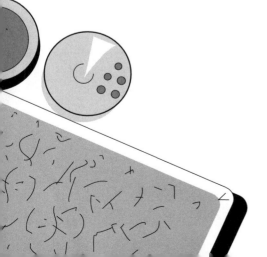

Browny's Seafood Teriyaki Marinade

3 garlic cloves, minced
1 C. light soy sauce
¹/₂ C. brown sugar
1 T. fresh ginger, grated
1 tsp. lemon juice

Mix all ingredients in medium plastic container. Cover and refrigerate.

Makes Marinade for 1 lb. of Seafood

CALCULATIONS BASED ON 4 SERVINGS

37 calories   0 gm total fat
0 gm saturated fat   0 mg cholesterol
608 mg sodium

Chef Scott's Wine Marinade

2 scallions, chopped
2 garlic cloves, minced
¹/₂ C. dry white wine
2 T. olive oil
1 T. light soy sauce
¹/₄ tsp. lemon-pepper
   seasoning

Mix all ingredients in medium plastic container. Cover and refrigerate.

Makes Marinade for 1 lb. of Seafood

CALCULATIONS BASED ON 4 SERVINGS

22 calories   2 gm total fat
0 gm saturated fat   0 mg cholesterol
37 mg sodium

Variations: dried herbs, such as thyme, marjoram, sage, rosemary, or basil

Cider Marinade

½ C. apple cider
2 T. Dijon mustard
2 T. olive oil
1 T. cider vinegar
1 tsp. sugar
1 tsp. dried sage
1 tsp. dried thyme
¼ tsp. red pepper flakes, crushed

Mix all ingredients in medium plastic container. Cover and refrigerate.

Makes Marinade for 1 lb. of Seafood

CALCULATIONS BASED ON 4 SERVINGS
24 calories   2 gm total fat
0 gm saturated fat   0 mg cholesterol
11 mg sodium

Hint: *Try freezing this marinade!*

Citrus Marinade

2 garlic cloves, minced
2 T. orange juice
2 T. light soy sauce
1 T. catsup
1 T. olive oil
1 T. lemon juice
1 T. fresh parsley, chopped

Mix all ingredients in medium plastic container. Cover and refrigerate.

Makes Marinade for 1 lb. of Seafood

CALCULATIONS BASED ON 4 SERVINGS
11 calories   1 gm total fat
0 gm saturated fat   0 mg cholesterol
87 mg sodium

Curried Yogurt Marinade

2 garlic cloves, peeled
1 ancho chili, seeded, chopped
1 C. low-fat plain yogurt
1 T. curry powder
$\frac{1}{4}$ tsp. salt
2 scallions, chopped

Mix garlic and chili in blender until finely chopped.
Add yogurt, curry powder, and salt. Blend until smooth.
Transfer to plastic bowl and stir in scallions. Cover and refrigerate.

Makes Marinade for 1 lb. of Seafood

CALCULATIONS BASED ON 4 SERVINGS

11 calories	0 gm total fat
0 gm saturated fat	1 mg cholesterol
51 mg sodium	

SPECIAL EQUIPMENT: blender

Herb Marinade

2 T. olive oil
$\frac{1}{2}$ C. red onion, minced
$\frac{1}{4}$ C. red wine vinegar
2 garlic cloves, minced
$\frac{1}{2}$ tsp. dried basil
1 bay leaf, crushed
$\frac{1}{4}$ tsp. salt

Mix all ingredients in medium plastic container. Cover and refrigerate.

Makes Marinade for 1 lb. of Seafood

CALCULATIONS BASED ON 4 SERVINGS

19 calories	2 gm total fat
0 gm saturated fat	0 mg cholesterol
37 mg sodium	

Lemon and Caper Marinade

1/4 C. olive oil
2 T. capers, finely chopped
1 tsp. lemon peel, finely grated
1 tsp. dried thyme
1/4 tsp. lemon-pepper seasoning

Mix all ingredients in medium plastic container. Cover and refrigerate.

Makes Marinade for 1 lb. of Seafood

CALCULATIONS BASED ON 4 SERVINGS
31 calories   3 gm total fat
0 gm saturated fat   0 mg cholesterol
44 mg sodium

Lemon and Lager Marinade

1 12-oz. bottle lager
3 garlic cloves, minced
2 T. olive oil
2 T. lemon juice
1 T. dried herbs, such as
    tarragon, oregano, or basil
1/4 tsp. salt

Mix all ingredients in medium plastic container. Cover and refrigerate.

Makes Marinade for 1 lb. of Seafood

CALCULATIONS BASED ON 4 SERVINGS
31 calories   3 gm total fat
0 gm saturated fat   0 mg cholesterol
44 mg sodium

Cabo San Lucas Marinade

3 garlic cloves, minced
1/3 C. lime juice
1/4 C. beer
1 T. fresh parsley, chopped
1 T. olive oil
2 tsp. Dijon mustard
1/2 tsp. ground cumin
1/4 tsp. each salt and pepper

Mix all ingredients in medium plastic container. Cover and refrigerate.

Makes Marinade for 1 lb. of Seafood

CALCULATIONS BASED ON 4 SERVINGS

14 calories	1 gm total fat
0 gm saturated fat	0 mg cholesterol
42 mg sodium	

Orange Marinade

2 T. orange juice
2 T. sweet rice vinegar
2 T. olive oil
1 T. Dijon mustard
1/4 tsp. each salt and pepper
2 garlic cloves, minced
1/2 tsp. dried basil

Mix orange juice, vinegar, oil, mustard, salt, and pepper. Add garlic and basil. Stir. Cover and refrigerate.

Makes Marinade for 1 lb. of Seafood

CALCULATIONS BASED ON 4 SERVINGS

19 calories	2 gm total fat
0 gm saturated fat	0 mg cholesterol
42 mg sodium	

Pineapple Teriyaki Marinade

3 garlic cloves, minced
3 T. pineapple juice (serve
    pineapple as a side dish and
    use the juice from the can)
3 T. light soy sauce
2 T. sherry
1 tsp. brown sugar
1 tsp. ground ginger
$^1/_2$ tsp. dry mustard

Mix all ingredients in medium
    plastic container. Cover and
    refrigerate.

Makes Marinade for 1 lb. of Seafood

CALCULATIONS BASED ON 4 SERVINGS
8 calories   0 gm total fat
0 gm saturated fat   0 mg cholesterol
125 mg sodium

Variations: *dash of ground red
    pepper; sesame seeds;
    scallions, shallots, or chives,
    chopped*

Rosemary and Apple Marinade

4 garlic cloves, minced
$^1/_4$ C. frozen apple juice
    concentrate, thawed
2 T. Dijon mustard
1 T. olive oil
1 T. dried rosemary
$^1/_4$ tsp. salt

Mix all ingredients in medium
    plastic container. Cover and
    refrigerate.

Makes Marinade for 1 lb. of Seafood

CALCULATIONS BASED ON 4 SERVINGS
19 calories   1 gm total fat
0 gm saturated fat   0 mg cholesterol
48 mg sodium

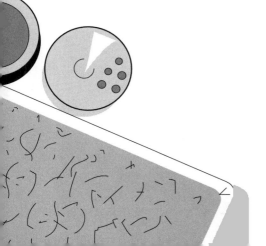

Thai Coconut Marinade

4 garlic cloves, minced
1 13$\frac{1}{2}$-oz. can low-fat coconut
    milk
2 T. fresh ginger, grated
2 T. lemongrass* (optional)
2 T. light soy sauce
2 T. dried cilantro
1 tsp. red pepper flakes,
    crushed

Mix all ingredients in medium
    plastic container. Cover and
    refrigerate.

Makes Marinade for 1 lb. of Seafood

CALCULATIONS BASED ON 4 SERVINGS
61 calories   6 gm total fat
5 gm saturated fat   0 mg cholesterol
81 mg sodium

This woody stalk is for flavoring only. Like a dried bay leaf, you can leave it in the cooking liquid or take it out before serving. Lemongrass adds a wonderful flavor. It is well worth the hunt!

Thymely Marinade

2 garlic cloves, minced
$\frac{1}{2}$ C. sweet onion, minced
$\frac{1}{2}$ C. lemon juice
2 T. olive oil
$\frac{1}{2}$ tsp. each dried thyme,
    oregano, and rosemary
$\frac{1}{4}$ tsp. each salt and pepper

Mix all ingredients in medium
    plastic container. Cover and
    refrigerate.

Makes Marinade for 1 lb. of Seafood

CALCULATIONS BASED ON 4 SERVINGS
20 calories   2 gm total fat
0 gm saturated fat   0 mg cholesterol
37 mg sodium

Wine Sauce Marinade

¹/₂ **C. dry white wine**
¹/₂ **tsp. dry mustard**
¹/₄ **C. lemon juice**
¹/₄ **tsp. lemon-pepper**
  seasoning

Mix all ingredients in medium
  plastic container. Cover and
  refrigerate.

Makes Marinade for 1 lb. of Seafood

CALCULATIONS BASED ON 4 SERVINGS
6 calories   0 gm total fat
0 gm saturated fat   0 mg cholesterol
5 mg sodium

Cajun Rub

¹/₂ **tsp. ground cumin**
¹/₂ **tsp. onion powder**
¹/₄ **tsp. red pepper flakes,**
  crushed
¹/₄ **tsp. garlic powder**

Combine all ingredients in small
  bowl. Store in an airtight
  container in a dry place.

Makes Rub for 1 lb. of Seafood

CALCULATIONS BASED ON 4 SERVINGS
3 calories   0 gm total fat
0 gm saturated fat   0 mg cholesterol
1 mg sodium

Caribbean Rub

1 T. ground ginger
1 T. garlic powder
½ T. ground cinnamon
½ tsp. ground allspice
½ tsp. ground cloves
½ tsp. salt
⅛ tsp. red pepper flakes, crushed

Combine all ingredients in small bowl. Store in an airtight container in a dry place.

Makes Rub for 2 lbs. of Seafood

CALCULATIONS BASED ON 8 SERVINGS
8 calories   0 gm total fat
0 gm saturated fat   0 mg cholesterol
146 mg sodium

Dill Rub

½ tsp. dried dill weed
½ tsp. dried parsley
⅛ tsp. celery salt
⅛ tsp. onion powder
⅛ tsp. garlic powder

Combine all ingredients in small bowl. Store in an airtight container in a dry place.

Makes Rub for 1 lb. of Seafood

CALCULATIONS BASED ON 4 SERVINGS
1 calories   0 gm total fat
0 gm saturated fat   0 mg cholesterol
64 mg sodium

Italian Seafood Rub

2 T. dried thyme
3 T. dried marjoram
3 T. dried basil
2 tsp. dried rosemary
2 tsp. dried oregano
$\frac{1}{4}$ tsp. each salt and pepper

Mix all ingredients in blender or cleaned coffee grinder. Process until finely chopped. Store in an airtight container in a dry place.

Makes Rub for 2 lbs. of Seafood

CALCULATIONS BASED ON 8 SERVINGS
21 calories   0 gm total fat
0 gm saturated fat   0 mg cholesterol
74 mg sodium

SPECIAL EQUIPMENT: blender

Beer Basting Sauce

1 C. beer
2 garlic cloves, minced
2 T. butter, melted
$\frac{1}{2}$ tsp. lemon-pepper seasoning
$\frac{1}{4}$ C. fresh parsley, minced

Mix beer, garlic, butter, and lemon-pepper seasoning in medium plastic container. Cover and refrigerate. Garnish seafood with parsley when ready to serve.

Serves: 4 (1 C.)

CALCULATIONS PER SERVING
20 calories   2 gm total fat
1 gm saturated fat   4 mg cholesterol
26 mg sodium

Honey Barbecue Basting Sauce

1 10$\frac{1}{2}$-oz. can condensed
   tomato soup
$\frac{1}{4}$ C. honey
2 T. Worcestershire sauce
2 T. olive oil
1 T. lemon juice
1 tsp. dry mustard
dash of hot pepper sauce

Combine all ingredients in saucepan. Boil. Reduce heat. Simmer uncovered for 5 minutes.

Serves: 4 (1$\frac{1}{2}$ C.)

CALCULATIONS PER SERVING

183 calories   8 gm total fat
1 gm saturated fat   0 mg cholesterol
594 mg sodium

SPECIAL EQUIPMENT: saucepan

Orange Barbecue Basting Sauce

$\frac{1}{2}$ C. Worcestershire sauce
$\frac{1}{4}$ C. orange juice
1 tsp. orange peel, grated
$\frac{1}{4}$ tsp. ground ginger

Mix all ingredients in medium plastic container. Cover and refrigerate.

Serves: 4 ($\frac{3}{4}$ C.)

CALCULATIONS PER SERVING

14 calories   0 gm total fat
0 gm saturated fat   0 mg cholesterol
73 mg sodium

Variations: fresh cilantro or thyme, minced; serrano or jalapeño peppers, chopped

Vinaigrette Basting Sauce

2 garlic cloves, minced
¼ C. white wine vinegar
2 T. water
2 T. olive oil
1 tsp. honey
1 tsp. ground cumin
¼ tsp. red pepper flakes, crushed
¼ tsp. each salt and pepper

Mix all ingredients in medium plastic container. Cover and refrigerate.

Serves: 4 (¾ C.)

CALCULATIONS PER SERVING
76 calories   7 gm total fat
1 gm saturated fat   0 mg cholesterol
148 mg sodium

Variations: fresh herbs such as basil and cilantro, chopped

Snappy Barbecue Sauce

¼ C. onion, minced
2 garlic cloves, minced
1 T. olive oil
1 8-oz. can tomato sauce
½ C. applesauce
1 T. vinegar
½ tsp. ground red pepper

Saute onion and garlic with olive oil in saucepan for 3 minutes. Add remaining ingredients. Simmer for 10 minutes. Serve hot.

Serves: 4 (2 C.)

CALCULATIONS PER SERVING
95 calories   6 gm total fat
1 gm saturated fat   0 mg cholesterol
345 mg sodium

SPECIAL EQUIPMENT: saucepan

Hint: Excellent served over grilled oysters or barbecued fish.

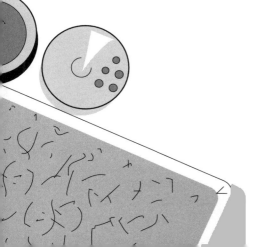

Chapter 12
Accompaniments

Compound Seasoned Butters

Seasoned butter is an easy way to flavor and enhance seafood when grilling. Make ahead and have on hand. Here are some tips.

- Blend an equal amount of butter and margarine.
- Soften butter mixture in a bowl.
- Blend the flavors with a spoon.
- Place the seasoned butter in the middle of a sheet of aluminum foil. Fold the top half over it, and form the seasoned butter into a log by rolling the foil into a uniform cylinder. Twist the ends of the foil. Refrigerate or freeze.
- Cut off a serving as you need. Seasoned butter will stay fresh in the freezer for several weeks if tightly wrapped.
- Slice off a pat of seasoned butter and melt over just-grilled seafood, or melt in the microwave and spoon over grilled seafood.
- Each seasoned butter recipe makes 24 teaspoons.

Compound seasoned butters are versatile and are equally delicious on grilled vegetables or breads. Wonderful to melt and use as a dipping sauce!

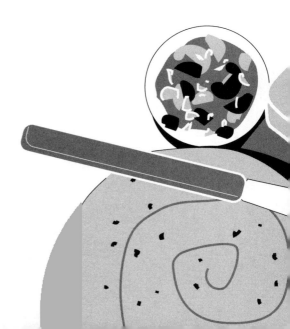

Pesto Butter

2 T. butter
2 T. margarine
$\frac{1}{2}$ C. fresh basil, minced
$\frac{1}{4}$ C. Parmesan cheese, grated
2 T. fresh parsley, minced
1 T. lemon juice
$\frac{1}{4}$ tsp. black pepper

Soften butter and margarine in bowl. Add all other ingredients. Blend flavors.

CALCULATIONS PER TEASPOON

22 calories	2 gm total fat
1 gm saturated fat	3 mg cholesterol
37 mg sodium	

Oriental Butter

$\frac{1}{4}$ C. butter
$\frac{1}{4}$ C. margarine
1 scallion, chopped
2 T. light soy sauce
1 T. lemon juice
1 tsp. sesame seeds, toasted
$\frac{1}{4}$ tsp. black pepper

Soften butter and margarine in bowl. Add all other ingredients. Blend flavors.

CALCULATIONS PER TEASPOON

37 calories	4 gm total fat
2 gm saturated fat	5 mg cholesterol
93 mg sodium	

Garlic-Ginger Butter

$\frac{1}{4}$ C. butter
$\frac{1}{4}$ C. margarine
2 garlic cloves, finely minced
1 T. fresh ginger, grated
1 T. lemon juice
dash of white pepper

Soften butter and margarine in bowl. Add all other ingredients. Blend flavors.

CALCULATIONS PER TEASPOON

36 calories	4 gm total fat
2 gm saturated fat	5 mg cholesterol
43 mg sodium	

Herb Butter

¼ C. butter
¼ C. margarine
2 garlic cloves, minced
1 T. fresh parsley, minced
1 T. lemon juice
1 T. fresh herbs, such as basil, oregano, or thyme, minced (or 1 tsp. dried herbs)

Soften butter and margarine in bowl. Add all other ingredients. Blend flavors.

CALCULATIONS PER TEASPOON

35 calories	4 gm total fat
2 gm saturated fat	5 mg cholesterol
43 mg sodium	

Jalapeño Butter

¼ C. butter
¼ C. margarine
2 jalapeño peppers, seeded, chopped
2 garlic cloves, minced
¼ C. fresh cilantro, chopped

Soften butter and margarine in bowl. Add all other ingredients. Blend flavors.

CALCULATIONS PER TEASPOON

36 calories	4 gm total fat
2 gm saturated fat	5 mg cholesterol
43 mg sodium	

Sun-Dried Tomato-Caper Butter

¼ C. butter
¼ C. margarine
½ C. sun-dried tomatoes, chopped
2 T. fresh parsley, minced
2 T. capers, minced
2 T. orange peel, grated

Soften butter and margarine in bowl. Add all other ingredients. Blend flavors.

CALCULATIONS PER TEASPOON

36 calories	4 gm total fat
2 gm saturated fat	5 mg cholesterol
70 mg sodium	

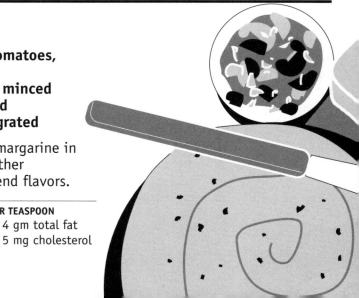

Lobster Butter Log

¼ C. butter
¼ C. margarine
½ lb. cooked lobster meat, finely chopped
½ C. fresh parsley, minced
1 tsp. onion, minced
½ tsp. lemon-pepper seasoning
¼ tsp. paprika

Soften butter and margarine in bowl. Add all other ingredients. Blend flavors.

CALCULATIONS PER TEASPOON

49 calories	4 gm total fat
2 gm saturated fat	14 mg cholesterol
72 mg sodium	

Hint: Place a slice of lobster butter over a grilled tuna, swordfish, or salmon fillet.

Basil Butter

¼ C. butter
¼ C. margarine
1 T. dried basil
1 tsp. white pepper
1 tsp. lemon-pepper seasoning

Soften butter and margarine in bowl. Add all other ingredients. Blend flavors.

CALCULATIONS PER TEASPOON

109 calories	12 gm total fat
4 gm saturated fat	5 mg cholesterol
99 mg sodium	

Hint: Serve with grilled oysters, clams, or mussels.

Mint Chutney

2 garlic cloves, chopped
1 jalapeño pepper, seeded,
 chopped
2 C. fresh mint
1 T. fresh ginger, chopped
2 T. sweet rice vinegar
1 T. olive oil
2 tsp. sugar
1/4 tsp. salt

Place garlic, jalapeño, mint, and
 ginger in medium plastic
 container. Mix.
Add vinegar, olive oil, sugar, and
 salt. Blend.

Serves: 4 (1/2 C.)

CALCULATIONS PER SERVING

58 calories   4 gm total fat
0 gm saturated fat   0 mg cholesterol
222 mg sodium

Pineapple Chutney

1 8-oz. can crushed pineapple
1/2 C. apple, chopped
1/2 C. red bell pepper, seeded,
 chopped
1/4 C. sweet onion, chopped
3 T. sugar
2 T. apple cider vinegar
1 tsp. mustard seed
1/4 tsp. salt

Mix all ingredients in a small
 saucepan. Simmer for 5
 minutes. Stir constantly.
Serve hot or cold.

Serves: 4 (2 C.)

CALCULATIONS PER SERVING

77 calories   0 gm total fat
0 gm saturated fat   0 mg cholesterol
147 mg sodium

SPECIAL EQUIPMENT: saucepan

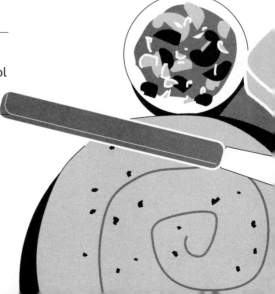

Wasabi Mayonnaise

1 tsp. wasabi powder
1 tsp. water
¼ C. light mayonnaise

Mix wasabi and water. Stir into a paste.
Fold mayonnaise into wasabi paste.

Serves: 4 (4 T.)

CALCULATIONS PER SERVING

53 calories	5 gm total fat
1 gm saturated fat	1 mg cholesterol
114 mg sodium	

Variations: Add 1 tsp. light soy sauce instead of water. A few drops of sesame or chili oil will add great flavor.

Black Bean Relish

3 garlic cloves, minced
3 jalapeño peppers, seeded, chopped
¼ C. onion, chopped
¼ C. celery, chopped
¼ C. carrot, chopped
2 T. olive oil
1 15-oz. can black beans, undrained
½ C. fresh cilantro, chopped
¼ tsp. salt

Sauté garlic, jalapeño, onion, celery, and carrot with olive oil in saucepan until tender.
Stir in black beans, cilantro, and salt. Bring to a boil. Reduce heat. Simmer uncovered for 10 minutes.
Serve hot.

Serves: 4 (2 C.)

CALCULATIONS PER SERVING

134 calories	7 gm total fat
1 gm saturated fat	0 mg cholesterol
587 mg sodium	

SPECIAL EQUIPMENT: saucepan

Corn Relish

3 Rojo garlic cloves, minced
2 C. frozen sweet corn
1 red bell pepper, seeded,
   chopped
1 green bell pepper, seeded,
   chopped
1 4-oz. can green chilies,
   chopped
2 T. lime juice
1 tsp. ground cumin

Mix all ingredients in large
   plastic bowl. Refrigerate until
   corn is thawed.
Serve chilled.

Serves: 4 (3 C.)

CALCULATIONS PER SERVING

89 calories	0 gm total fat
0 gm saturated fat	0 mg cholesterol
62 mg sodium	

Avocado and Jalapeño Salsa

1 ripe avocado
1 sweet onion, chopped
1 jalapeño pepper, seeded,
   chopped
¼ C. fresh parsley, chopped
1 C. light sour cream
¼ tsp. lemon-pepper seasoning

*Hint: Excellent served with
grilled shrimp!*

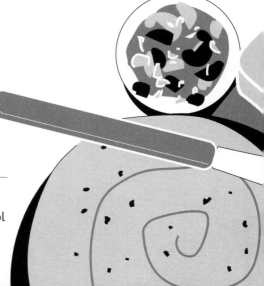

Cut avocado in half and remove
   pit. Scoop out avocado meat.
   Cut into cubes.
Place avocado meat in bowl with
   onion, jalapeño pepper, and
   parsley. Mix.
Gently fold sour cream and
   lemon-pepper seasoning into
   avocado mixture.

Serves: 4 (2 C.)

CALCULATIONS PER SERVING

178 calories	13 gm total fat
5 gm saturated fat	20 mg cholesterol
140 mg sodium	

Green Tomato Pickle Relish

Yes! Finally, a tasty way to get rid of green tomatoes!

1 C. green tomatoes, chopped
1 red bell pepper, seeded,
chopped
1 green bell pepper, seeded,
chopped
1 sweet onion, chopped

PICKLING SAUCE
1 C. apple cider vinegar
1 T. brown sugar
1 tsp. dry mustard
1 tsp. celery salt
¼ tsp. salt

Mix vegetables in large glass
bowl.
Mix all Pickling Sauce ingredients
in saucepan. Simmer for 10
minutes. Cool.
Add sauce to vegetables. Cover
and refrigerate.

Serves: 4 (4 C.)

CALCULATIONS PER SERVING

63 calories	0 gm total fat
0 gm saturated fat	0 mg cholesterol
397 mg sodium	

SPECIAL EQUIPMENT: saucepan

Roasted Red Pepper Salsa

1 7-oz. jar roasted red peppers,
drained, chopped
¼ C. black olives, chopped
¼ C. Parmesan cheese,
shredded
4 T. fresh parsley, chopped
1 T. olive oil
¼ tsp. lemon-pepper
seasoning

Mix all ingredients in medium
plastic container. Cover and
refrigerate.

Serves: 4 (1½ C.)

CALCULATIONS PER SERVING

79 calories	6 gm total fat
2 gm saturated fat	4 mg cholesterol
324 mg sodium	

Cranberry Salsa

**1 8-oz. can whole cranberry
    sauce**
¹/₄ C. picante sauce
¹/₄ C. orange juice
1 tsp. orange zest
¹/₂ tsp. dried oregano

SPECIAL EQUIPMENT: saucepan

Mix all ingredients in saucepan.
    Bring to a boil. Reduce heat.
    Simmer 10 minutes.
Serve hot.

Serves: 4 (¹/₃ C.)

CALCULATIONS PER SERVING
94 calories   0 gm total fat
0 gm saturated fat   0 mg cholesterol
121 mg sodium

Crunchy Apple Salsa

**1 large Anaheim chili pepper,
    seeded, chopped**
2 C. apples, chopped
¹/₂ C. sweet onion, chopped
¹/₄ C. lime juice
2 T. fresh cilantro, chopped
**¹/₄ tsp. lemon-pepper
    seasoning**

Mix all ingredients in medium
    plastic container. Cover and
    refrigerate.

Serves: 4 (3 C.)

CALCULATIONS PER SERVING
55 calories   0 gm total fat
0 gm saturated fat   0 mg cholesterol
22 mg sodium

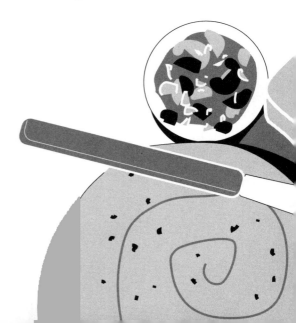

Cucumber Salsa

1 cucumber, cut in half
    lengthwise, seeded, thinly
    sliced
2 T. red bell pepper, seeded,
    finely chopped
1 T. sweet rice vinegar
$1/2$ tsp. sugar
$1/4$ tsp. dried dill weed
$1/4$ tsp. lemon-pepper
    seasoning

Mix all ingredients in medium plastic container. Cover and refrigerate.

Serves: 4 ($1/3$ C.)

CALCULATIONS PER SERVING

14 calories	0 gm total fat
0 gm saturated fat	0 mg cholesterol
22 mg sodium	

Orange Salsa

2 oranges, peeled, cut into
    $1/2$" pieces
1 small sweet onion, chopped
1 jalapeño pepper, seeded,
    finely chopped
$1/4$ C. fresh cilantro, chopped
2 T. lime juice
2 T. olive oil
$1/4$ tsp. salt

Mix all ingredients in medium plastic container. Cover and refrigerate.

Serves: 4 (2 C.)

CALCULATIONS PER SERVING

106 calories	7 gm total fat
1 gm saturated fat	0 mg cholesterol
218 mg sodium	

Peach Salsa

2 peaches, diced
2 plums, diced
$1/4$ C. raisins
$1/4$ C. sweet onion, diced
1 T. fresh mint, chopped
1 T. lemon juice

Mix all ingredients in medium plastic container. Cover and refrigerate.

Serves: 4 (1 C.)

CALCULATIONS PER SERVING

69 calories	0 gm total fat
0 gm saturated fat	0 mg cholesterol
2 mg sodium	

Pear-Pepper Salsa

2 pears, diced
2 scallions, sliced
1 jalapeño pepper, seeded,
    diced
1/4 C. red bell pepper, seeded,
    diced
1/4 C. raisins
1 T. sweet rice vinegar

Mix all ingredients in medium
    plastic container. Cover and
    refrigerate.

Serves: 4 (2 C.)

CALCULATIONS PER SERVING

81 calories   0 gm total fat
0 gm saturated fat   0 mg cholesterol
73 mg sodium

Salsa Fresca

1 serrano chili, seeded, minced
1/2 C. tomato, minced
1/4 C. sweet onion, minced
1/4 C. cucumber, diced
1 T. olive oil
1/4 tsp. salt
dash of hot pepper sauce

Gently mix all ingredients in
    medium plastic container.
    Cover and refrigerate.

Serves: 4 (1 C.)

CALCULATIONS PER SERVING

41 calories   4 gm total fat
0 gm saturated fat   0 mg cholesterol
150 mg sodium

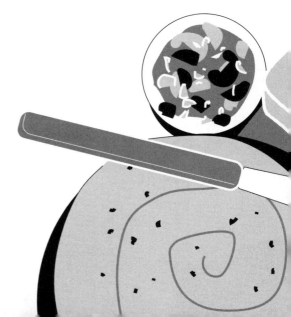

Thanksgiving Salsa

1½ C. Craisins™, chopped
1 jalapeño pepper, seeded, minced
¼ C. scallion, sliced
¼ C. fresh cilantro, chopped
2 T. lime juice
2 tsp. fresh ginger, grated
¼ tsp. salt

Mix all ingredients in medium plastic container. Cover and refrigerate.

Serves: 4 (⅓ C.)

CALCULATIONS PER SERVING

168 calories	0 gm total fat
0 gm saturated fat	0 mg cholesterol
224 mg sodium	

Hint: *Fresh or frozen sugared cranberries may be used instead of Craisins™.*

Louisiana Cocktail Sauce

½ C. light mayonnaise
½ C. catsup
¼ C. chili sauce
¼ C. horseradish
1 tsp. Worcestershire sauce
1 tsp. lemon juice
¼ tsp. hot pepper sauce
dash of garlic salt
dash of onion salt

Mix all ingredients in medium plastic container. Cover and refrigerate.

Serves: 8 (1½ C.)

CALCULATIONS PER SERVING

77 calories	5 gm total fat
1 gm saturated fat	0 mg cholesterol
463 mg sodium	

Simple, Delicious Cocktail Sauce

1 C. light sour cream
1 C. light mayonnaise
$^1/_2$ C. picante sauce
$^1/_4$ C. lemon juice

Mix all ingredients in medium plastic container. Cover and refrigerate.

Serves: 4 (2$^1/_2$ C.)

CALCULATIONS PER SERVING

295 calories	25 gm total fat
8 gm saturated fat	20 mg cholesterol
736 mg sodium	

Zesty Cocktail Sauce

1 8-oz can tomato sauce
2 T. chili sauce
$^1/_2$ tsp. hot pepper sauce
$^1/_4$ tsp. sugar
$^1/_4$ tsp. dried thyme
$^1/_8$ tsp. dried basil
$^1/_8$ tsp. dried oregano

Combine all ingredients in saucepan. Simmer for 10 minutes.
Serve hot or cold.

Serves: 4 (1 C.)

CALCULATIONS PER SERVING

27 calories	0 gm total fat
0 gm saturated fat	0 mg cholesterol
446 mg sodium	

SPECIAL EQUIPMENT: saucepan

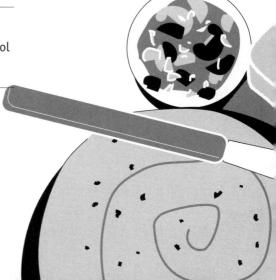

Sweet and Sour Dipping Sauce

2 garlic cloves, minced
3 T. honey
3 T. fresh parsley, minced
2 T. lemon juice
2 T. olive oil
¼ tsp. salt
dash of hot pepper sauce

Mix all ingredients in medium plastic container. Cover and refrigerate.

Serves: 4 (½ C.)

CALCULATIONS PER SERVING

113 calories
1 gm saturated fat
149 mg sodium

7 gm total fat
0 mg cholesterol

Teriyaki Dipping Sauce

½ C. light soy sauce
3 T. dried sage
2 T. water
1 T. peanut oil
1 tsp. sugar
1 tsp. fresh ginger, grated
1 tsp. sweet rice vinegar

Mix all ingredients in medium plastic container. Cover and refrigerate.

Serves: 4 (¾ C.)

CALCULATIONS PER SERVING

48 calories
1 gm saturated fat
303 mg sodium

3 gm total fat
0 mg cholesterol

Addie's Tartar Sauce

At our wedding 30 years ago, we served a seafood banquet of barbecued salmon and Petersburg, Alaska shrimp with this tartar sauce. The sauce is still requested by relatives and friends. Addie is a wonderful friend and mother-in-law.

1 C. fat-free Miracle Whip™
2 T. dill pickle, finely chopped
1 T. sweet onion, grated
1 T. lemon juice
¹/₄ tsp. celery salt

Mix all ingredients in medium plastic container. Cover and refrigerate.

Serves: 4 (1 C.)

CALCULATIONS PER SERVING
83 calories   0 gm total fat
0 gm saturated fat   0 mg cholesterol
962 mg sodium

Mango Tartar Sauce

¹/₄ C. light mayonnaise
¹/₄ C. light sour cream
2 T. mango, peeled, diced
2 T. sweet onion, minced
1 T. fresh mint, minced
1 T. orange juice

Mix all ingredients in medium plastic container. Cover and refrigerate.

Serves: 4 (³/₄ C.)

CALCULATIONS PER SERVING
79 calories   6 gm total fat
2 gm saturated fat   5 mg cholesterol
121 mg sodium

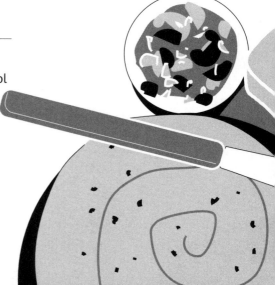

Tarragon Tartar Sauce

¹/₄ **C. light mayonnaise**
¹/₄ **C. low-fat plain yogurt**
2 T. Dijon mustard
1 tsp. dried tarragon
¹/₈ **tsp. each salt and black pepper**

Blend ingredients in small plastic container.

Serves: 4 (¹/₂ C.)

CALCULATIONS PER SERVING

70 calories 6 gm total fat
1 gm saturated fat 1 mg cholesterol
308 mg sodium

Hint: *Brush seafood with sauce during grilling.*

Bibliography

Alder, K., Welch, R., and Wells, C. *Hooked on Fish on the Grill*. Kansas City, Missouri: Pig Out Publications, 1992.

Barnard, M. *Low-fat Grilling*. New York: HarperCollins, 1995.

Bonomo, G. *The Great Book of Seafood Cooking*. Trans. by S. Harris. New York: International Culinary Society, 1990 (originally published 1989).

Fraser, M. *The Random House Barbecue and Summer Foods Cookbook*. Toronto: Madison Press Books, 1989.

Howard, M. *All Fired Up!* Ontario, Canada: Firefly Books, 1998.

Maine, M., ed. "Keeping Safe," in *Simply Perfect Grilling* 1999, pp. 10-11. 1999.

Peterson, J. *Fish and Shellfish*. New York: William Morrow, 1996.

Reader, T., and Sloan, K. *The Sticks and Stones Cookbook*. Toronto: Macmillan Canada, 1999.

Redmayne, P., ed. *Simply Seafood, Summer 1992,* 1992.

Spieler, M. *The Classic Barbecue and Grill Cookbook*. New York: DK Publishing, 1996.

Time Life Books. *Fish*. Alexandria, Virginia: Time Life Books, 1979.

Time Life Books. *Indoor Grilling: Great Tips and Recipes for Grilling in the Oven and on the Stove*. Hong Kong: Time Life Books, 1997.

Weber-Stephen Products. *Weber's Art of the Grill: Recipes for Outdoor Living*. San Francisco: Chronicle Books, 1999.

Williams, C., ed. *Williams-Sonoma Lifestyles: Backyard Barbecues*. Singapore: Time Life Books, 1999.

Yoshida, S. *Seafood Cooking for Your Health*. Tokyo: Japan Publications, 1989.

Resources

American Cancer Society
1-800-ACS-2345
www.cancer.org

American Diabetes Association
1-800-232-3472
www.diabetes.org

American Heart Association
1-800-242-8721
www.americanheart.org

Consumer Products Safety Commission
1-800-638-2772
www.cpsc.gov

National Hotline of the American Dietetic Association
1-800-366-1655
www.eatright.org
    (nutrition professionals)

Food and Drug Association (FDA):
Food Information and Seafood Hotline
1-800-332-4010
Center for Food Safety & Applied Nutrition Outreach & Information Center
(202) 205-5251
www.cfsan.fda.gov
www.nal.usda.gov/fnic/foodcomp
    (nutritional data on food)

Recipe Index

Main Dishes

Marinades, Rubs, and Sauces

Accompaniments

Subject Index

This index is intended to be used as a cross reference. Entries are listed under categories and by types of fish that may be substituted in any given recipe.

For example, under **Shrimp** there is a kabob recipe for **Shrimp on a Stick**. This recipe also appears under **Lobster**, as slipper tail lobster is one of the possible seafood substitutions for that recipe.

Subject Index

Subject Index

Subject Index

Subject Index

Subject Index

Ordering Information

Please send me _____ copies of

    Seafood Grilling Twice a Week   @ $14.95 ea.   _____

    Seafood Twice a Week   @ $14.95 ea.   _____

Washington residents add sales tax (8.6%) $1.29 ea.   _____

Shipping and Handling $3.50   _____

    TOTAL   _____

Method of Payment: ☐ Check   ☐ Money Order

    ☐ Visa   ☐ Mastercard

    ☐ Discover   ☐ American Express

Name of Cardholder _____

Account # _____ Expires _____

Signature _____

Bill to:

Name _____

Address _____

City _____ State _____ Zip _____

Phone _____ Email _____

Fax _____

Ship to:

Name _____

Address _____

City _____ State _____ Zip _____

Mail payment to: National Seafood Educators

    P.O. Box 60006

    Richmond Beach, WA 98160

    Phone: (206) 546-6410   Fax: (206) 546-6411

Please list bookstores, gift shops, or seafood markets in your area that would be interested in handling this book.

Name   Phone

_____   _____

_____   _____

_____   _____